An Unofficial Harry Potter Fan's Cookbook

An Unofficial Harry Potter Fan's Cookbook

Spellbinding Recipes for Famished Witches and Wizards

AURÉLIA BEAUPOMMIER

Translated by Grace McQuillan
Photography by Aline Shaw

Racehorse Publishing

Racehorse Publishing books may be purchased in bulk at special discounts for sales promotion, corporate gifts, fund-raising, or educational purposes. Special editions can also be created to specifications. For details, contact the Special Sales Department, Racehorse Publishing, 307 West 36th Street, 11th Floor, New York, NY 10018 or info@skyhorsepublishing.com.

Racehorse Publishing™ is a pending trademark of Skyhorse Publishing, Inc.®, a Delaware corporation.

Visit our website at www.skyhorsepublishing.com.

10 9 8 7 6 5

Library of Congress Control Number: 2019912313

Cover design by Brian Peterson
Cover image credit: Getty Images

ISBN: 978-1-63158-602-6
eBook ISBN: 978-1-63158-606-4

Printed in China

PROCLAMATION

Educational Decree
NO. 11-52

The Ministry reminds all first-year wizards that the use of magic is forbidden outside of school.

As such, an adult and/or **N.E.W.T.** level wizard is strongly encouraged to be present in order to supervise the use of certain objects to perform potentially dangerous acts and to ensure that slicing, transfers, and cooking are done without cuts, burns, or various explosions.

It is also highly advisable to use the necessary protective spells and equipment.

The Ministry would like to remind the reader (and/or legal representatives) that it is his or her responsibility to ensure both one's individual safety and that of one's guests, in particular those suffering from food allergies as well as pregnant women and witches.

The author and her representatives will not be held responsible in the event of hospitalization in the Non-Magical Wound Care or Experimental Spells Units.

On behalf of the Ministry of Magic:
A. Beaupommier

CONTENTS

UNOFFICIAL RECIPES INSPIRED BY

PRIVET DRIVE

Dudley's Hamburger Special

Ingredients

Serves 4

1 onion

1 ounce (30 g) butter

4 beef patties, 18 ounces (500 g)

8 slices of bacon

Pinch of sugar

2 tomatoes

8 lettuce leaves

4 pickles

4²/₅ ounces (125 g) grated cheddar cheese

4 hamburger buns

Mustard, ketchup

This recipe is perfect for people with a voracious appetite . . . just like Harry's cousin Dudley!

Preparation Time • 20 minutes ◆ *Cooking Time* • 25 minutes

◆ Preheat your oven to 250°F (120°C, th. 3-4).

◆ Cast an anti-crying spell and peel the onion. Then slice it into rounds and cook the rounds for 20 minutes in a small pan over medium heat with a little water.

◆ Melt the butter in a frying pan and cook the beef patties 4 minutes on each side. Keep them warm in the oven.

◆ Rinse the frying pan with the help of a cleaning spell of your choice and use it again to cook the bacon until it is crispy.

◆ Remove any excess grease by sponging the bacon with a paper towel and keep warm in the oven.

◆ When the onion rounds are transparent, add the pinch of sugar and let caramelize for a few minutes. Set aside and keep warm.

◆ Wash the tomatoes, cut them into rounds, remove the juice and seeds, and set aside.

◆ Rinse the lettuce leaves and gently dry, then dry off the pickles as well and slice them. Toast the buns with a dragon-breath spell (or a toaster).

◆ Spread one side of each bun with ketchup and the other with mustard, then, with a simple consolidation spell, assemble the burger in the following order: bottom half of the bun, first lettuce leaf, burger patty, cheddar, bacon, onion rings, tomato, second lettuce leaf, pickle slices, and finally the other half of the bun.

◆ Serve nice and warm.

Uncle Vernon's Favorite Dessert

EQUIPMENT

1 cake mold

1 mixer

1 baking tray and 1 sheet of parchment paper

1 pair of dragon-hide gloves

INGREDIENTS

Serves 4

Cake:

One 4-ounce (125 g) container of plain unsweetened yogurt

2 yogurt containers of flour

⅛ ounce (3.5 g) yeast

1 yogurt container of sugar

½ yogurt container of oil

3 eggs

Hazelnut Spread (makes 10 ounces, or 300 g):

3½ ounces (100 g) hazelnuts

3½ ounces (100 g) almonds

4½ ounces (130 g) granulated sugar

1 teaspoon water

3½ ounces (100 g) powdered sugar

¾ ounce (20 g) whole milk powder

1 ounce (30 g) cocoa

⅖ ounce (10 g) sunflower oil

Uncle Vernon is not a role model: cake is meant to be eaten, not used as a hammer.

Preparation Time • 10 minutes + 20 minutes

Cooking Time • 45 minutes + 30 minutes

To prepare the cake:

◆ Preheat your oven to 350°F (180°C, th. 6–7) and pour the yogurt into a large bowl. Keep the yogurt container on hand and clean it out with a cleaning spell of your choice. You will use it to measure the rest of the ingredients.

◆ Sift the flour and yeast into the bowl, then add the sugar and mix until combined. Next add the eggs (without the shells) and then the oil.

◆ Pour the batter into your mold and bake for 40–45 minutes depending on your oven.

◆ The cake is done baking if you can stick your wand (or a knife) into the center and it comes out dry.

To make the hazelnut spread:

◆ Lower the oven temperature to 300°F (150°C, th. 5–6).

◆ Line the baking tray with the parchment paper and spread the hazelnuts and almonds over it. Place the tray in the oven 20–25 minutes until the nuts are a pretty golden color (or use a dragon-breath spell).

◆ In a pan, bring the sugar and water to a boil then lower the heat and allow to cook 2–3 minutes. Pour in the hazelnuts and almonds and toss with your wand (or a wooden spoon) until the mixture is brown. (It is normal for a white shell to form around the nuts. With heat it will melt and caramelize.)

◆ Next add the powdered sugar, powdered milk, cocoa, and oil, and mix again.

◆ Put on your dragon-hide gloves and pour the contents of the pot onto the parchment-lined baking tray. Spread out the mixture and allow to cool 20 minutes. Pour this preparation into

(continued)

the mixer and mix for a few minutes until you reach your desired consistency. Be careful: the more you mix, the more like a liquid the spread will become.

◆ Transfer the spread to containers and store in the refrigerator.

◆ Slice enough cake for all of your guests and serve with the hazelnut spread for dipping.

Aunt Petunia's Masterpiece

EQUIPMENT

1 round cake pan
(9 inches, 24 cm)

1 Bundt pan (9½ inches, 24 cm)

(or two other molds with the
same dimensions)

INGREDIENTS

Serves 6

Cookie Base:

12¾ ounces (350 g) flour

¼ ounce (7 g) yeast

3½ ounces (100 g) cornstarch

8 ounces (225 g) butter

6⅕ ounces (175 g) granulated
sugar

Topping:

8⅘ ounces (250 g) red berries

1 packet of strawberry jello (see
section on Shopping)

8⅘ ounces (250 g) whipped
cream

1¾ ounces (50 g) candied violets

Handful of mint leaves

*A delicious dessert, perfect for impressing important guests . . .
at least if Dobby doesn't smash it to the ground first.*

Preparation Time • 10 minutes + 30 minutes
Cooking Time • 20–25 minutes

◆ Preheat your oven to 350°F (180°C, th. 6–7) and begin the
cookie base.

◆ Sift the flour and cornstarch into a bowl with a twirl of your
wand and add the yeast. In a separate bowl, mix together the
softened butter and the sugar. Pour the wet mixture over the flour
and mix again.

◆ Pour the batter into the round cake pan, smooth it out, and
bake 20–25 minutes until the cookie is a pale golden color.

◆ Let cool before removing from the mold and set aside.

◆ Rinse and dry the berries and remove any stems.

◆ Stir the jello powder into 10 fluid ounces (300 ml) of
simmering water then add 10 fluid ounces (300 ml) of cold water
(or follow the instructions given by the manufacturer) and then
pour the jello into the Bundt pan, add the berries, and let set in
the refrigerator for 30 minutes. To remove from the mold: run
the base of the mold under warm water for a few seconds and
carefully remove it.

**You can assemble the dessert in the following manner, but
don't hesitate to use a simple consolidation spell:**

◆ Place the cooled cookie base on the serving dish followed by the
fruit jello.

◆ Fill the hole in the middle with whipped cream and continue
coating the jello to form a whipped cream pyramid.

◆ Sprinkle with candied violets and mint leaves and serve without
waiting too long. (Levitation charms should be avoided when
transporting this dessert.)

Unofficial Recipes Inspired By

Breakfast at Hogwarts

Pumpkin Juice

INGREDIENTS

makes 1 pitcher

34 fluid ounces (1 l) apple juice

8⅘ ounces (250 g) fresh
   pumpkin flesh (frozen if out
   of season)

4⅖ ounces (125 g) apricot jam

1 wand tip of cinnamon
   (= 1 pinch)

Served at every meal!

Preparation Time • 5 minutes

◆ Pour all of the ingredients except the cinnamon into a standard model cauldron of medium size and combine with swirl of your wand (or an immersion blender) until the mixture has a uniform consistency.

◆ Add the pinch of cinnamon and serve chilled.

Porridge

INGREDIENTS

serves 4

17 fluid ounces (½ l) milk

6¾ fluid ounces (20 cl) water

1 cinnamon stick

7 ounces (200 g) rolled oats

1 Granny Smith apple

Drizzle of lemon juice

2 tablespoons of honey from the
    Forbidden Forest

Handful of crushed hazelnuts

Preparation Time • 10 minutes + 10 minutes

Cooking Time • 5 minutes

◆ Heat the milk and water with the cinnamon stick in a cauldron over low heat.

◆ Sprinkle in the oats and stir clockwise for 5 minutes until the mixture is soft.

◆ Remove the cinnamon stick with a Levitation charm.

◆ Rinse and peel the apple, then cut it into thin pieces. Drizzle with lemon juice, mix well, and set aside.

◆ Stir the honey into the oats with a mixing spell, pour into a bowl, top with the apples and hazelnuts, and enjoy.

Orange Jelly

INGREDIENTS

makes 4 jars of 8⁴/₅ ounces (250 g) each)

2¹/₅ pounds (1 kg) oranges not treated with growth serum

1 lemon not treated with No-Pest Spray

2¹/₅ pounds (1 kg) jam sugar for 25¹/₃ fluid ounces (750 ml) fruit juice

There's nothing like a stack of excellent slices of toast with jelly to build strength before a Quidditch match.

Preparation Time • 20 minutes   ◆   *Cooking Time* • 7 minutes

◆ Place a small plate in the freezer.

◆ Rinse the oranges and the lemon and then, using a Severing charm (or a citrus peeler), remove the peels.

◆ Place the peels in a pot of water, blanch for 5 minutes, and drain.

◆ Juice the oranges and lemon and weigh the juice.

◆ Calculate the amount of sugar you will need based on the following proportion: 2¹/₅ pounds (1 kg) sugar for 25¹/₃ ounces (750 ml) juice.

◆ Stir the juice in a copper cauldron (standard model, size 2), bring to a boil, and cook for 4–7 minutes depending on the directions on your container of sugar.

◆ The jelly is ready when a drop poured onto the cold plate remains congealed long enough to count to ten.

◆ Add the peels and stir counterclockwise, then store in jars for one week before tasting.

Breakfast for a Wizard Waking Up on the Right Side of the Bed

INGREDIENTS

serves 4

4 eggs

8 slices of bacon

4 tomatoes

1¾ ounces (50 g) butter

1 bunch parsley from the Hogwarts garden

2¹/₁₀ ounces (60 g) breadcrumbs

2¹/₅ pounds (1 kg) mushrooms from the Forbidden Forest

1 bouquet of fine herbs (parsley, chives, tarragon, chervil, etc.), finely chopped

Salt and pepper

Preparation Time • 20 minutes   ◆   *Cooking Time* • 20 minutes

◆ Crack the eggs into a cup and pour them gently into a frying pan, arranging the white evenly around the yolk with a gentle flick of your wand (or a wooden spoon). Cook over high heat 3–4 minutes until the edges start to become crispy.

◆ Heat a large nonstick pan and fry the bacon slices a few seconds on each side until they are quite brown then set them aside to keep warm.

◆ Preheat the oven to 350°F (180°C, th. 6–7).

◆ Rinse the tomatoes, cut them in half, lightly salt them, and let them dry on a towel.

◆ Warm up the butter in a frying pan, add the tomatoes, and cook 2 minutes on each side over high heat.

◆ Rinse and chop the parsley.

◆ Place the tomatoes in a baking dish, cut side up, and stuff with parsley and breadcrumbs. Add a pat of butter and bake 10–15 minutes until the tomatoes have softened to your liking.

◆ Remove the sandy stems from the mushrooms and quickly clean them with a cleaning spell of your choice (or a damp towel). Next, peel and cut them in thin slivers.

◆ Melt the butter in a frying pan and sauté the mushrooms quickly over high heat for around 5 minutes.

◆ Sprinkle with finely chopped herbs and serve hot.

◆ Place the eggs on top of the bacon and serve along with the tomatoes and mushrooms.

UNOFFICIAL RECIPES INSPIRED BY

HARRY'S FAVORITE FOODS

Treacle Tart

An excellent recipe for Harry's favorite dessert!

EQUIPMENT

1 cake ring 8 inches (20 cm) in diameter

1 jar dried beans or peas

INGREDIENTS

serves 8

Dough:

7 ounces (200 g) flour

1²/₅ ounces (40 g) butter

1 egg

Pinch of salt

3–4 tablespoons of water taken from the Great Lake on a moonless night

Filling:

15¹/₅ fluid ounces (450 ml) golden syrup (see section on Shopping)

2¹/₁₀ ounces (60 g) butter

Juice of 1 lemon

5¹/₃ ounces (150 g) plain unsweetened corn flakes

Preparation Time • 20 minutes + 30 minutes   ◆   *Cooking Time* • 1 hour

◆ Sift the flour into a large bowl with 1²/₅ ounces (40 g) butter cut into pieces and incorporate using the tips of your fingers. When the mixture resembles cornmeal, add the egg and salt. If the mixture seems too dry, add in a bit of water.

◆ Mix again, roll into a ball, cover in plastic wrap and let rest 30 minutes in the refrigerator.

◆ Preheat the oven to 350°F (180°C, th. 6–7).

◆ Roll out the dough to a thickness of 2 mm with a steady sweep of your wand and place into the greased cake ring. Poke holes in the bottom of the tart with a fork or the tip of your wand (be sure to clean it afterwards!).

◆ Place a sheet of parchment paper on top of the dough, fill with dried beans or peas, bake for 20 minutes, then remove the parchment paper and dried beans or peas.

◆ Lower the oven temperature to 325°F (160°C, th. 6).

◆ In a small cauldron over low heat, melt the golden syrup then add the pieces of butter and the lemon juice. Remove from heat and add the corn flakes. Mix and pour over the bottom of the tart.

◆ Bake for 20 minutes, lower the temperature to 275°F (140°C, th. 5), then continue cooking 15–20 minutes longer until the crust is golden, and the filling is soft.

◆ Let cool and serve with whipped cream.

Mini Steak and Kidney Pies

EQUIPMENT

1 mini tart pan

1 cookie cutter of your choice (star, etc.) around ¾-inch (2 cm) wide

(see section on Techniques for Non-Magical People)

INGREDIENTS

serves 6

1 ox kidney

1²⁄₃ pounds (750 g) beef steak

1 ounce (30 g) flour or cornstarch

4²⁄₅ ounces (125 g) mushrooms from the Forbidden Forest

Juice of 1 lemon

1 tablespoon oil

1 ounce (30 g) butter

1 onion

2 tablespoons Worcestershire sauce

1 tablespoon tomato paste

4²⁄₅ fluid ounces (130 ml) non-alcoholic dark beer

8½ fluid ounces (250 ml) beef broth

1 teaspoon thyme

1 bay leaf

7 ounces (200 g) shortcrust pastry

6¹⁄₅ ounces (175 g) puff pastry

1 beaten egg

Preparation Time • 30 minutes • *Cooking Time* • 45 minutes

◆ Remove the kidney membrane with a Severing charm, cut into eight pieces, and remove the fibrous and fatty portions.

◆ Cut the beef in small cubes. Pour the flour (or cornstarch) into a freezer bag, add the beef and the kidney pieces then seal the bag and gently shake to coat all of the meat in flour.

◆ After confirming that your mushrooms are edible (and that none of them bite), clean them off with a damp towel and remove the sandy stems. Peel and cut into slivers and drizzle with the lemon juice to keep them from turning brown.

◆ Heat the oil and butter in a cauldron with a thick base.

◆ Cast an anti-crying charm and peel the onion. Cut into thin strips and cook them for 5 minutes over high heat until soft before removing them from the pan and replacing them with the beef and kidney pieces. Next add the Worcestershire sauce, tomato paste, beer, beef broth, mushrooms, thyme, and bay leaf. Bring to a boil and let simmer for 1 hour until the meat is tender.

◆ Preheat the oven to 350°F (180°C, th. 6–7).

◆ Roll out the pastry doughs. Line the mini tart molds with shortcrust pastry up to the rim, then fill with the meat mixture. (Don't forget to remove the bay leaf!)

◆ Use the puff pastry to create a cover for each mini tart, making sure that the dough extends beyond the edge of each mold by about 1 cm.

◆ With a cookie cutter, cut out small shapes in the center of the puff pastry cover so that air can escape, then carefully place one on top of each mini tart and seal the edges by pressing down gently (or by casting a Sticking charm).

◆ Brush with the beaten egg and bake for 45 minutes.

UNOFFICIAL RECIPES INSPIRED BY

A PARTY IN THE COMMON ROOM

Canary Creams

EQUIPMENT
4 ramekins

INGREDIENTS
serves 4

2 gelatin sheets

2 tablespoons lemon juice

8⁴/₅ ounces (250 g) liquid crème fraîche

1¾ ounces (50 g) sugar

2¹/₁₀ ounces (60 g) ground almonds

1 ounce (30 g) lemon peel, not treated with growth serum or No-Pest Spray

Unlike Fred and George's successful joke, these delicious treats will not make you sprout feathers.

Preparation Time • 20 minutes + 1 hour resting time

Cooking Time • 5 minutes

◆ Soften the gelatin sheets in a bowl of water for 15 minutes.

◆ Place a small cauldron over low heat.

◆ Pour in the lemon juice, crème fraîche, and sugar. Mix well.

◆ Next add the ground almonds and the lemon peels and stir again with a mixing spell while imitating the song of the canary (this step is absolutely essential to the success of this recipe).

◆ Wring out the gelatin sheets by pressing them gently between your hands and add them to the cauldron.

◆ Fill the ramekins, recite a plumage spell with the seriousness required, and chill for 1 hour.

Authentic Cold Butterbeer (alcohol free)

INGREDIENTS

serves 4

2 fluid ounces (60 ml)
   butterscotch syrup (see section
   on Shopping)

cream soda (see section on
   Shopping)

Whipped cream, if desired

*The best thing after an evening of hard work
at 12 Grimmauld Place.*

Preparation Time • 5 minutes

◆ With a languid sweep of your wand, pour the butterscotch syrup into mugs followed by chilled cream soda.

◆ Stir gently, top with a generous helping of whipped cream, and enjoy.

Authentic Warm Butterbeer (alcohol free)

INGREDIENTS

serves 4

17 fluid ounces (½ l) milk

2 fluid ounces (60 ml)
   butterscotch syrup (see section
   on Shopping)

Whipped cream (not overly
   beaten) if desired

*Drink this creamy beverage to ward off the chill
of the dreariest winter day.*

Preparation Time • 5 minutes   ◆   *Cooking Time* • 5 minutes

◆ Warm the milk in a standard model cauldron.

◆ Pour the milk into mugs, then add the syrup and stir gently with your wand (or a spoon).

◆ Add the whipped cream if desired and serve immediately.

Victory Cake

EQUIPMENT

1 square cookie cutter 4 inches (10 cm) on each side

(see section on Techniques for Non-Magical People)

1 sheet pan

Parchment paper

INGREDIENTS

serves 6

Cake:

4 eggs

$4^{2}/_{5}$ ounces (125 g) sugar

$4^{2}/_{5}$ ounces (125 g) flour

$4^{2}/_{5}$ ounces (125 g) butter

1 jar of jam in your desired color

Toppings:

Gryffindor, Ravenclaw, and Slytherin Houses:

$5^{1}/_{3}$ ounces (150 g) powdered sugar

2 tablespoons lemon juice

2 drops of food coloring: beet juice, spinach juice, or blueberry juice

Hufflepuff House:

$2^{1}/_{10}$ ounces (60 g) crème fraîche

$4^{2}/_{5}$ ounces (125 g) baking chocolate

Preparation Time • 5 minutes + 15 minutes resting time

Cooking Time • 10 minutes

◆ Depending on which House wins the match or the House Cup, Dobby and the other house-elves change the filling for the cake: redcurrant jelly for Gryffindor House, blueberry jam for Ravenclaw House, rhubarb jam for Slytherin House, and hazelnut spread for Hufflepuff House (see recipe p. 5).

◆ Preheat your oven to 400°F (200°C, th. 7–8).

◆ In a bowl, beat together the sugar and eggs until the mixture doubles in volume and is very foamy. Use a frothing spell if necessary or an electric beater.

◆ Incorporate the flour by sifting it with a twirl of your wand.

◆ Butter the parchment paper and place it on the sheet pan. Next spread the dough over the sheet pan with an unfurling spell and bake 10 min.

◆ Let cool 15 minutes.

◆ Remove the parchment paper and use the cookie cutter to cut out the cake layers. Spread each cutout with jam in the color of your choosing and pile them on top of each other to form a small tower similar to those that hold the cheering fans.

◆ Prepare the toppings in the following manner: Gryffindor, Slytherin, and Ravenclaw Houses: combine all of the ingredients and pour over the top. Hufflepuff House: melt the chocolate with the crème fraîche over very low heat and pour over the dessert.

◆ Let dry for a few minutes and serve with butterbeer (p. 25) or pumpkin juice (p. 11).

A LETTER FROM NEVILLE'S UNCLE

My dear Neville,

I received the letter your owl delivered to me and read all about the start of school at Hogwarts this year. I am very glad you are enjoying yourself so much in that beautiful old castle.

I want to reiterate that the Potions classes are absolutely necessary, and that no one can be excused from going to them just because he or she is terrified of the professor.

Because I myself experienced a bit of apprehension going to certain classes, I am enclosing the recipe for Hardy Sweets for you.

These explosive little treats are packed full of audacity and were of great help long ago to your grandmother Augusta and I by giving us the courage we needed to "get back on the broom," as we say.

I am certain that you will soon be the pride of all of your professors and if this is not the case, comfort yourself with the knowledge that it will be true one day.

Your loving uncle,
Algie

Hardy Sweets

EQUIPMENT
A square or rectangular dish
   lined with parchment paper

INGREDIENTS
makes around 30 sweets

Ingredients for Wizards:
Mimbulus sap

Ubull purée

Medusa's cackle

Moon ray powder

Comet dust

**Ingredients for Non-Magical
People:**
8½ fluid ounces (250 ml)
   cactus water (see section on
   Shopping)

8⁴/₅ ounces (250 g) unsweetened
   applesauce

¾ ounce (20 g) pectin

1²/₅ pounds (650 g) sugar

1¾ ounces (50 g) sparkling sugar

Effect:
Provides a guaranteed feeling of exceptional
bravery to whoever ingests it.

Side Effects:
Lowers ability to correctly assess risks.

Preparation Time • 15 minutes   ◆   *Cooling Time* • 2 hours

◆ Cast a Shield charm to avoid squirts of stinksap, and collect
the Mimbulus sap with extreme caution and in an appropriate
container (bowl, mountain troll skull, small cauldron approved
by the Ministry, etc.).

◆ Pour the Ubull purée (applesauce) into a large copper cauldron
and add the Mimbulus sap (cactus juice), Medusa's cackle
(pectin), and the Moon ray powder (sugar).

◆ Stir gently and bring to a boil, moving your wand first in
the direction that takes you back in time, then in the opposite
direction, and finally in the shape of the infinity symbol (non-
magical people call it a "figure-eight").

◆ Repeat the stirring pattern until the mixture forms large foamy
bubbles.

◆ Wait 7 minutes.

◆ Put on dragon-hide gloves or oven mitts and pour the mixture
onto the dish lined with parchment paper and let cool without
touching the mixture again.

◆ After two hours, slice the hardened mixture into ²/₃-inch
(1.5 cm) cubes and roll them in the comet dust (sparkling sugar)
until they have a generous coating.

◆ Eat one whenever you find yourself lacking courage.

UNOFFICIAL RECIPES INSPIRED BY

THE HALLOWEEN BANQUET

Pumpkin Soup

EQUIPMENT

1 immersion blender

1 steam cooker or 1 standard size cauldron

INGREDIENTS

serves 4

2$^1/_5$ pounds (1 kg) various squashes (pumpkin, butternut, Hungarian blue, etc.)

1 chicken bouillon cube

Nutmeg

Salt and pepper

2$^1/_{10}$ ounces (60 g) thick crème fraîche

The use of Hagrid's enchanted pumpkins is not recommended.

Preparation Time • 30 minutes   ◆   *Cooking Time* • 45 minutes

◆ With sharp swipes of your wand, chop the squashes into large chunks and remove the seeds.

◆ If you are using a cauldron, put on your dragon-hide gloves and carefully remove the squash skins, then place the pieces of squash in your cauldron, cover with water, crumble the bouillon cube, and cook for 45 minutes, until the squash is tender.

◆ If you are using a steam cooker, dissolve the bouillon cube in the water bowl then place the pieces of squash in the basket without removing the skin. Cook for 45 minutes, until the flesh is tender and the tip of your wand can easily poke through it. Cool for a few minutes and remove the skin by gently pulling on it, or with a Severing charm.

◆ Taste and add grated nutmeg, salt, and pepper as desired.

◆ Blend the pieces of squash with a little of the cooking broth until your soup has a smooth texture. Pour into bowls, add the crème fraîche, and serve hot.

Halloween Vegetables

Preparation Time • 30 minutes   ◆   *Cooking Time* • 1 hour

INGREDIENTS

serves 6

2$\frac{1}{5}$ pounds (1 kg) potatoes

2$\frac{1}{5}$ pounds (1 kg) parsnips

2$\frac{1}{5}$ pounds (1 kg) carrots

2$\frac{1}{5}$ pounds (1 kg) onions

2$\frac{1}{5}$ pounds (1 kg) squash from
   the Hogwarts garden

2 tablespoons oil

1$\frac{3}{4}$ ounces (50 g) butter

Salt and pepper

Dobby thinks it is a very good idea to cook these vegetables in large quantities. They are delicious, and if there are any left over (which rarely happens) they freeze quite well.

◆ Preheat your oven to 350°F (180°C, th. 6-7).

◆ Rinse and peel the potatoes, parsnips, carrots, and onions, then chop them into large cubes with sharp swipes of your wand. Carefully remove the skin of the squash and remove the seeds before cutting it into pieces in the same way.

◆ Place all of the vegetables in an ovenproof dish, drizzle with the oil, and toss to make sure all of the vegetables are coated. Sprinkle with chunks of butter and put in the oven.

◆ After 30 minutes, stir the vegetables with your wand (or a wooden spatula) and continue cooking.

◆ When the vegetables are fully cooked, they should be golden and crispy on the outside and tender on the inside.

◆ Season with salt and pepper and serve warm.

Pumpkin Pie

EQUIPMENT
1 tart pan, 10 inches (25 cm) wide

INGREDIENTS
serves 6

For the dough:
8 ounces (225 g) flour

Pinch of salt

3½ ounces (100 g) butter

6¾ fluid ounces (20 cl) water

For the filling:
1 pound (450 g) precooked squash (red kuri, butternut, etc.)

OR 2⅕ pounds (1 kg) pumpkin

5⅓ ounces (150 g) light brown sugar

½ teaspoon ground cinnamon

½ teaspoon ground ginger

½ teaspoon grated nutmeg

Pinch of salt

3 eggs

8½ fluid ounces (250 ml) milk

Make sure to finish your slice before the Headmaster announces it's time for bed!

Preparation Time • 15 minutes + 30 minutes of resting time

Cooking Time • 45 minutes

◆ If you are using raw pumpkin, carefully remove the skin and seeds and slice it in large chunks. Place in a pot, cover with water, and cook for around 45 minutes until the flesh is tender.

◆ Preheat your oven to 400°F (200°C, th. 7-8).

◆ With a twirl of your wand, sift the flour and salt into a bowl and add the butter after cutting it into small pieces. Combine using the tips of your fingers until the mixture has a grainy texture.

◆ Incorporate the water until the dough forms a soft ball.

◆ Refrigerate for 10 minutes.

◆ Roll out the dough with a steady sweep of your wand and carefully lay it in your tart pan. Refrigerate again for 20 minutes.

◆ Prepare the filling by mixing the pumpkin flesh with the sugar, cinnamon, ginger, nutmeg, and salt. In another bowl, beat together the eggs and milk and add to the pumpkin spice mixture.

◆ Stir the ingredients together with a mixing spell, pour into the tart pan, and bake.

◆ After 15 minutes, lower the temperature of the oven to 350°F (180°C, th. 6) and continue baking for 30–40 minutes until your wand comes out smooth when you plunge it into the pie.

◆ Let cool as long as you can and enjoy.

Hogwarts-Style Beef Wellington

EQUIPMENT

1 cookie cutter of your choice for decorating

(see section on Techniques for Non-Magical People)

INGREDIENTS

serves 6

9/10 ounce (25 g) butter

1 tablespoon neutral-flavored oil (sunflower, etc.)

1 round or rump roast 1¾–2⅕ pounds (800 g–1 kg)

3½ ounces (100 g) mushrooms from the Forbidden Forest

1 tablespoon fresh parsley

18 ounces (500 g) puff pastry

2⅔ ounces (75 g) liver pâté

Salt and pepper

1 beaten egg (for egg wash)

Preparation Time • 20 minutes ◆ *Cooking Time* • 50 minutes

◆ Preheat your oven to 415°F (210°C, th. 7–8).

◆ In a large frying pan, melt the butter and oil together over high heat. Place the roast in the pan and cook for 4 min on each side until every side is a nice golden-brown color.

◆ With a Levitation spell, transfer the roast to an ovenproof dish and cook for 15 minutes.

◆ Remove the roast from the oven, cover in aluminum foil, and let cool for at least 20 minutes.

◆ After making sure that none of the mushrooms bite, clean them off with a damp towel (or a cleaning spell of your choice) then peel them and cut into slivers. Cook the mushrooms for 5 minutes in the same pan used for the roast then sprinkle with chopped parsley, salt, and pepper.

◆ Set aside around 3½ ounces (100 g) of pastry dough for decoration and roll out the rest into a rectangle large enough to wrap around the roast beef.

◆ Spoon the mushrooms onto the center of the pastry in a row, following the longer edge. Next place the roast on top of the mushrooms and finish by spreading the liver pâté over the meat.

◆ Fold down the pastry dough to wrap the roast in an elegant bundle, making sure the edges are folded underneath.

◆ Roll out the remainder of the dough and cut out shapes of your choice (pumpkin, Sorting Hat, broom, star, etc.) and place the shapes on top of your bundle, using a Sticking charm or a little water to help them stay in place.

◆ Brush with the beaten egg and bake for 30 minutes until the pastry is golden and crispy.

UNOFFICIAL RECIPES INSPIRED BY

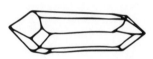

THE DEATHDAY PARTY

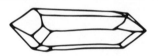

Troll Toe Crunch

INGREDIENTS

serves 6

4–6 herb sausages (depending on their size)

1 puff pastry

2 drops green food coloring (spinach juice)

1 drop red food coloring (beet juice)

1 drop blue food coloring (blueberry juice)

20–25 whole almonds

2 tablespoons milk

Preparation Time • 30 minutes ◆ *Cooking Time* • 15 minutes

◆ Preheat your oven to 350°F (180°C, th. 6–7).

◆ With sharp swipes of your wand, cut the sausages into roughly 2-inch (5 cm) pieces.

◆ Roll out the puff pastry dough, add the food coloring, and knead the dough to evenly distribute the colors.

◆ Add more food coloring if needed, respecting the same proportions, until you have achieved the color of troll toes—in other words, a color that is totally undefinable.

◆ Place a piece of sausage on the pastry dough and cut out a long rectangle around it, leaving an extra ¾ inch (2 cm) for the toenail.

◆ Roll the sausage up inside the pastry by folding the edges.

◆ Place a whole almond on the edge of the toe and press down gently to form the toenail (if you sprinkle it with sugar, you will have a shiny nail)

◆ With your wand, or a small knife, make a few small incisions in the middle of the toe where the joint would be.

◆ Brush with milk and bake for 15–20 minutes.

Aged Bones

Moldy food may taste better for ghosts,
but it is not recommended for consumption by the living.

EQUIPMENT

1 mold for bone-shaped candies
  or chocolates (see section on
  Shopping)

OR see section on Techniques
  for Non-Magical People

INGREDIENTS

serves 6

7 ounces (200 g) bread

18 ounces (500 g) white meat
  (turkey, chicken, etc.)

8½ fluid ounces (¼ l) milk

8⁴/₅ ounces (250 g) crème fraîche

4 eggs

7 ounces (200 g) chinese
  artichokes from the Hogwarts
  garden (if not in season, use
  soybean sprouts instead)

Preparation Time • **10** minutes ◆ *Cooking Time* • **1** hour

◆ Preheat your oven to 350°F (180°C, th. 6–7).

◆ Using a dragon-breath spell (or a toaster), lightly toast
the bread until it is very dry but not yet brown. Then, with a
crumbling spell, grind the toast into breadcrumbs.

◆ In a bowl, mix together the meat, milk, crème fraîche, eggs,
and breadcrumbs. Pour the mixture into the molds and bake for
around 1 hour until the tip of a knife or your wand comes out
clean after stabbing the center of the bone.

◆ Let cool and remove from mold.

◆ Clean and rinse the artichokes then cook them in a cauldron
of boiling water until they are tender. Carefully dry them off and
place them on the serving dish. If using, rinse and dry the soybean
sprouts in the same way.

◆ If you used a loaf pan, cut a little bit off the sides to create a
bone shape.

◆ Place each serving on a bed of artichokes or soybean sprouts
and consume in a funereal manner.

Delicious Eyes

EQUIPMENT
A transparent glass for each guest

INGREDIENTS
serves 6

1 can whole pitted lychees

1 bunch red grapes (if out of
  season, use prunes instead)

34 fluid ounces (1 l) raspberry
  juice

Preparation Time • 10 minutes

◆ Drain the lychees with a drying spell (or a colander) and set
aside the juice (it might be useful to you later).

◆ Rinse the grapes, then stuff one in each lychee to form the
pupil of the eye.

◆ Place the eyes in the glasses and fill with raspberry juice.

◆ Serve chilled.

R·I·P· Cookies

EQUIPMENT

1 tombstone-shaped cookie
   cutter

(see chapter on Techniques for
   Non-Magical People)

INGREDIENTS

serves 4

4²/₅ ounces (125 g) flour

1 egg

2¹/₁₀ ounces (60 g) sugar

1 tablespoon vanilla extract

2¹/₁₀ ounces (60 g) butter

Preparation Time • 10 minutes + 30 minutes of resting time
Cooking Time • 10-15 minutes

◆ Preheat your oven to 350°F (180°C, th. 6–7).

◆ With a twirl of your wand, sift the flour into a bowl, add the egg (without the shell), sugar, and vanilla extract and mix together.

◆ Cast a Hot Air charm to soften the butter without melting it.

◆ Stir everything together with a mixing spell until you have a smooth dough. Roll the dough into a ball, cover it in plastic wrap, and refrigerate for 30 minutes.

◆ Roll out the dough to a thickness of around 3–5 mm: use either a rolling pin or a steady sweep of your wand.

◆ Cut out the cookies with your cookie cutter and bake for around 10–15 minutes until they are a pale blond color but not yet golden brown.

◆ Remove the cookies from the oven, let cool, and serve.

UNOFFICIAL RECIPES INSPIRED BY

CHRISTMAS AT HOGWARTS

Leftover Turkey Sandwiches

INGREDIENTS

serves 4

8 slices whole wheat bread

1 bunch fresh spinach leaves

3½ ounces (100 g) walnuts

18 ounces (500 g) cold cooked turkey (either from a whole roasted turkey or turkey cutlets)

1 jar of cranberry chutney (see section on Shopping)

This filling treat is perfect after a snowball fight in the Hogwarts courtyard.

Preparation Time • 10 minutes

◆ With the assistance of a dragon-breath spell, toast the slices of bread.

◆ Rinse the spinach leaves, then carefully dry them and remove any stalks that are a little tough, if necessary.

◆ Use a crushing spell to crush the walnuts into large pieces.

◆ Cast a finger-shield charm and cut the turkey in thin slices or cubes, depending on your preference.

◆ Divide the ingredients equally four ways to make four sandwiches.

◆ Spread the chutney on the slices of bread (one side only).

◆ On one slice of bread sprinkle some of the walnut pieces, half of the spinach leaves, and the turkey, followed by the rest of the spinach, the rest of the walnuts, and lastly the second slice of toasted bread.

◆ Press down gently to pack everything together and serve with a large glass of pumpkin juice (p. 11) or divination tea (p. 67)

Christmas Tartlets

EQUIPMENT
1 mini tart pan

1 star-shaped cookie cutter (or see section on Techniques for Non-Magical People)

INGREDIENTS
makes 24 mini tarts

10²/₃ ounces (300 g) flour

1 ounce (30 g) ground almonds

6 ounces (170 g) butter

2⁴/₅ ounces (80 g) sugar

Peel from 1 lemon not treated with growth serum or No-Pest Spray

1 beaten egg

3 tablespoons milk

2 tablespoons powdered sugar (for decoration)

1 jar of mincemeat (see section on Shopping)

Preparation Time • 15 minutes + 30 minutes of resting time

Cooking Time • 15-20 minutes

Dobby knows that Hogwarts students are crazy about these tartlets. This is why he always makes a lot of them at once. They also freeze very well.

◆ Sift the flour into a bowl, then add the ground almonds and butter after cutting it into small pieces. Combine using the tips of your fingers, then by rubbing your hands together.

◆ Next pour in the sugar and lemon peel and continue incorporating with your hands or a mixing spell until your mixture has a cornmeal-like texture.

◆ In a separate bowl, beat together the egg and milk, then add to the previous mixture and beat until you have a smooth and uniform dough. Roll the dough into a ball, cover with plastic wrap, and refrigerate for 30 minutes.

◆ Preheat your oven to 400°F (200°C, th. 7–8).

◆ Roll out the dough on a lightly floured surface and cut out 48 circles with a spin of your wand, or a glass (24 circles for the bases of the tarts, and 24 for the tops).

◆ Place 24 of the circles into your mini tart molds followed by 1 teaspoon of mincemeat per tart.

◆ With your cookie cutter, cut out the shape of your choice from the circles that will be used to top the tarts. Make sure the shapes are slightly larger than the molds because the dough will shrink as it bakes.

◆ Place the tops of your tarts over the mincemeat, brush with a little milk, and bake for 15–20 min until the tartlets are a pretty golden-brown color. (*You are strongly advised not to enlist the help of a dragon, even one that is considered tame.*)

◆ Sprinkle with powdered sugar and serve.

Elf Socks

Socks are a must-have at Christmastime, especially for Dobby.

EQUIPMENT

2 sock-shaped cookie cutters of two different sizes

(see section on Techniques for Non-Magical People)

2 sheets of parchment paper

INGREDIENTS

makes around 25 shortbread cookies

$4^2/_5$ ounces (125 g) softened butter

$4^2/_5$ ounces (125 g) sugar

1 teaspoon vanilla extract

$8^4/_5$ ounces (250 g) flour

Pinch of salt

1 egg

1 jar of your favorite jam (or orange jelly, p. 15)

Decorations according to your personal inspiration: bright red icing with broom motifs, green icing decorated with flecks of gold, etc.

Preparation Time • 10 minutes + 30 minutes of resting time

Cooking Time • 15 minutes

◆ In a bowl, cream the butter and sugar until the mixture becomes foamy. Add the vanilla extract, sifted flour, salt, and egg. Combine using a mixing spell.

◆ Spinning your wand in a quick, concentric motion, roll the dough into a ball, then cover in plastic wrap and refrigerate for 30 minutes.

◆ Preheat your oven to 350°F (180°C, th. 6–7).

◆ With a steady sweep of your wand, roll out the dough on a lightly floured surface to a thickness of about 2–3 mm. With your larger cookie cutter, cut out 50 socks.

◆ Place 25 of the socks on a sheet of parchment paper and bake for 10–15 minutes until they are a pale golden color.

◆ Put on your dragon-hide leather gloves, take the sock cookies out of the oven, slide the sheet of parchment paper onto a rack, and let the cookies cool.

◆ While the first batch of cookies is cooling, use your smaller cookie cutter to cut smaller socks out of the larger ones (save the extra dough from these small socks to make additional cookies).

◆ Place the emptied socks on the second sheet of parchment paper and bake the same way you baked the first batch.

◆ Once the sock cookies have completely cooled, remove them from the parchment paper.

◆ Place one spoonful of jam on the whole socks and top with the empty sock.

◆ Decorate however you please with dots of frosting, powdered sugar, or tiny pine trees made of sugar. Enjoy in good company.

Christmas Pudding

EQUIPMENT

1 steamed pudding mold

1 red-checkered dish towel (the pudding will not have quite the same taste if the checks are a different color)

Aluminum foil

Parchment paper

INGREDIENTS

serves 6

7¼ ounces (185 g) butter, separated

13¼ ounces (375 g) granulated sugar

3 eggs

8⅘ ounces (250 g) flour

1 teaspoon baking soda

2⅘ ounces (80 g) candied cherries, cut in pieces

2⅘ ounces (80 g) candied apricots, cut in pieces

2⅘ ounces (80 g) candied pineapple chunks, cut in pieces

2¹⁄₁₀ ounces (60 g) candied citrus peel

2¹⁄₁₀ ounces (80 g) chopped walnuts

Powdered sugar for decoration

2¹⁄₁₀ ounces (60 g) dates, cut in pieces

2¹⁄₁₀ ounces (60 g) raisins

Preparation Time • 20 minutes • *Cooking Time* • 4 hours

Dobby prepares this cake well in advance because it can be kept in the freezer until the moment is right.

◆ In a bowl, mix 6½ ounces of softened butter with the sugar until you have a mousse-like consistency, then add the eggs (without their shells), continuing to stir.

◆ Sift in the flour and baking soda. Then, using a Levitation spell, add the candied fruit and the chopped walnuts and stir again.

◆ Cut one sheet of parchment paper, butter it, and place it on the bottom of your pudding mold. Next, prepare one sheet each of aluminum foil and parchment paper and grease both of them. Place the sheet of aluminum foil butter side up on the counter. Then place the sheet of parchment paper on top of it, butter side up.

◆ Pour your mixture into the mold and cover with the two sheets, placing the buttered sheet of parchment paper on top of the mold first. The sheet of aluminum foil should therefore be on top.

◆ Cover with a clean towel that you can hold in place with a knotting spell or a piece of string. Then, wrap the entire mold in the red-checkered dish towel and tie the two ends together to form a handle you will use to transfer the mold.

◆ Place an upturned saucer in a cauldron and place the mold wrapped in the dish towel on top of it. Fill the cauldron halfway with water.

◆ Boil for 4 hours, regularly adding very hot water to keep the cooking from stopping.

◆ After 4 hours, remove the pudding from the cauldron with a Levitation spell. Watch out: it will be very heavy, very hot, and there will be boiling water on the dish towel. Use an apron made of dragon-hide or cast a waterproofing charm over the dish.

(continued)

◆ Let cool, untie the dish towel, cut the thread, remove the sheets of parchment paper and aluminum foil, and flip the pudding over onto a plate. Tap the bottom of the mold three times with your magic wand while reciting an unsticking spell and remove the mold.

◆ Sprinkle with powdered sugar and serve warm with a nice hot cup of tea.

Hogwarts-Style Snowballs

EQUIPMENT
1 whisk
Plastic wrap

INGREDIENTS
serves 4

O.W.L. Level Wizards:
4 egg whites
Pinch of salt
1 jar vanilla custard
2 tablespoons milk
Powdered sugar for decoration

N.E.W.T. Level Wizards:
4 egg whites
Pinch of salt
1 vanilla bean
8½ fluid ounces (¼ l) whole milk
2 egg yolks
1¾ ounces (50 g) granulated sugar
Powdered sugar for decoration

Preparation and Cooking Time • 5 minutes + 20 minutes

For all wizards:
◆ Crack the eggs and pour the whites into a bowl with a pinch of salt. Cast a frothing spell or use an electric beater to beat the whites into stiff peaks. The whites are ready when you can turn the bowl over above your head without finding yourself wearing a white and moussey hat.

◆ Next, place a sheet of plastic wrap in a separate bowl, leaving plenty of extra hanging over the edge. Pour in one quarter of the beaten egg whites and close the plastic wrap over them to form a small ball. Microwave for 30–45 seconds until firm.

◆ Repeat the same process to make 4 snowballs. Let cool.

◆ Cut the snowballs in half, and using a small spoon or a Gouging spell scoop out the center of four of the half-spheres, leaving a border three-quarters of an inch (2 cm) thick to prevent any unwanted holes.

Preparation of the custard for O.W.L. level wizards:
◆ Dilute the vanilla custard with the milk.

Preparation of the custard for N.E.W.T. level wizards:
◆ Cut the vanilla bean in half lengthwise. With the back of a knife, scrape the two halves to remove the seeds.

◆ Place a standard model cauldron over high heat with an upturned saucer on the bottom (this will keep the milk from sticking to the bottom of the cauldron). Pour in the milk and bring to a boil, watching carefully. You can use one of your professor's favorite mottos: "Constant vigilance!"

◆ Pour the egg yolks and sugar into a bowl, whisk until the mixture turns white, and add a small amount of the boiling milk a little at a time. (This is to heat up the eggs without scrambling them.)

◆ Lower the heat and pour this mixture back into your cauldron of boiling milk, adding the vanilla seeds and bean. Stir with a wooden spoon and cook at very low heat for 5 minutes.

(continued)

◆ To check if the custard is ready, stir then immediately run your finger through the leftovers on the back of the spoon. The custard is thick enough if the line you traced is still visible. If this is not the case, cook for a little bit longer.

For all wizards:
◆ Place the hollow half of each snowball on a plate, fill with vanilla custard, and cover with the other half-sphere.

◆ Sprinkle with powdered sugar and enjoy immediately.

UNOFFICIAL RECIPES INSPIRED BY

THE PROFESSORS' FAVORITES

Hagrid's Rock Cakes

EQUIPMENT
Sheet pan (or oven baking tray)

Parchment paper

INGREDIENTS
serves 4

3½ ounces (100 g) whole hazelnuts

3½ ounces (100 g) baking chocolate

3½ ounces (100 g) sugar

1 egg

3½ ounces (100 g) flour

A fantastic recipe for Hagrid's homemade treat . . . be careful not to break your teeth!

Preparation Time • 5 minutes ◆ *Cooking Time* • 20 minutes

◆ Preheat your oven to 350°F (180°C, th. 6–7).

◆ Using a crushing spell, break the hazelnuts and chocolate into large pieces.

◆ In a bowl, mix the sugar and egg together, then add the chocolate and hazelnuts.

◆ Sift in the flour with a twirl of your wand and stir and stir some more until everything is combined.

◆ Line the sheet pan with a sheet of parchment paper. Scoop small balls of dough onto the paper, keeping some space between each one (they will spread out during baking).

◆ Bake for 20 minutes. For tougher cookies, bake for another 10 minutes.

 # The First Birthday Cake

EQUIPMENT
1 cake pan (round if possible)

1 small piping bag or cone (see section on Techniques for Non-Magical People)

INGREDIENTS
serves 6

Cake:

7 ounces (200 g) baking chocolate

6⅓ ounces (180 g) butter

6 eggs

Pinch of salt

3½ ounces (100 g) flour

6⅓ ounces (180 g) sugar

Icing:

5⅓ ounces (150 g) powdered sugar

1 tablespoon lemon juice

Red and green food coloring (beet juice and spinach juice)

A yummy recreation of Harry's first ever birthday cake.

Preparation Time • 20 minutes ◆ *Cooking Time* • 45 minutes

◆ Preheat the oven to 350°F (180°C, th. 6–7).

◆ Place a large cauldron filled with water on the fire.

◆ With the help of a crushing spell, break the chocolate into large pieces, then cut the butter into cubes. Pour the chocolate and butter into a small cauldron that you will place on top of the larger one so the heat of the water can gently melt the butter and chocolate together.

◆ Stir regularly with your wand (be sure to clean it afterwards).

◆ Crack the eggs, set aside the yolks, and pour the whites into a bowl with a pinch of salt. Cast a frothing spell or use an electric beater and beat the egg whites into stiff peaks. The egg whites are ready when you can turn the bowl upside down above your head without finding yourself suddenly wearing a white and foamy hat.

◆ Sift the flour into a separate bowl (use a quick twirl of your wand), then add the sugar, egg yolks, and chocolate mixture and combine. Next add the beaten egg whites little by little, trying not to stir too much in order to keep as much air in your batter as possible.

◆ Pour the batter into your mold and bake for around 45 minutes.

◆ The cake is baked through when the tip of your wand (or your knife) comes out dry after poking the center of the cake.

◆ Let cool and carefully remove from the pan either by hand or with a Levitation charm.

◆ While the cake is cooling, prepare the icing by dissolving the powdered sugar in the lemon juice. Set aside 2–3 tablespoons of icing in a small bowl.

◆ Add a few drops of beet juice to the first bowl of icing and mix until it is as pink as a Puffskein's tongue. Use the spinach juice

(continued)

and repeat the process for the small batch of icing. Aim for a "moss growing on the north side of the hut" green.

◆ Combine a Levitation spell with a languid sweep of your wand and cover the (cooled) cake with the pink icing. Smooth out the icing and allow to dry for a few minutes.

◆ Fill your piping bag with green icing and draw your best "*Happy Birthday*" for an unforgettable birthday cake . . .

Professor McGonagall's Ginger Newts

EQUIPMENT

1 newt-shaped cookie cutter

(see sections on Shopping and Techniques for Non-Magical People)

INGREDIENTS

makes 30 cookies

1¾ ounces (50 g) candied ginger

6⅓ ounces (180 g) flour

4¼ ounces (120 g) softened butter

3⅕ ounces (90 g) sugar

½ teaspoon vanilla extract

1 tablespoon orange juice

The Transfiguration professor's sweet treat—perfect for rewarding students who rebel against corrupt professors.

Preparation Time • 30 minutes   •   *Cooking Time* • 10-5 minutes

◆ Preheat your oven to 350°F (180°C, th. 6–7).

◆ Cast a finger-shield charm and with sharp swipes of your wand (or a knife), cut the ginger into small cubes.

◆ In a bowl, sift the flour and add the butter, sugar, vanilla, and orange juice, and when the mixture is smooth, add the small cubes of ginger.

◆ With a steady sweep of your wand, roll out the dough before cutting out your newts with the cookie cutter.

◆ Line a baking sheet with parchment paper, arrange the newts on the tray, and bake for 10–15 minutes until the cookies are a pale golden color and crispy.

◆ Let cool and store in an airtight container.

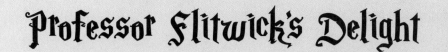

Professor Flitwick's Delight

EQUIPMENT
1 paper cocktail umbrella for
decoration

INGREDIENTS
serves 4
²/₃ fluid ounce (20 ml) cherry
syrup

17 fluid ounces (½ l) cola

3½ ounces (100 g) vanilla ice
cream

Candied cherries

*The Charms professor can look forward to this ice-cold drink at
The Three Broomsticks, even in the dead of winter.*

Preparation Time • 5 minutes

◆ Pour the cherry syrup into glasses and add the cola, combining
everything using a gentle mixing spell.

◆ Carefully add one scoop of vanilla ice cream to each glass.

◆ Place a few candied cherries on top of the ice cream, decorate
with an umbrella, and serve immediately.

The Headmaster's Password

EQUIPMENT
1 ice cream popsicle mold (or any individual mold of your choice)

INGREDIENTS
makes 6 ice cream popsicles

18 ounces (500 g) sugar

8½ fluid ounces (¼ l) water from the Great Lake

17 fluid ounces (500 ml) lemon juice

18 ounces (500 g) whipped cream

Preparation Time • 10 minutes + 6 hours of resting time

◆ Pour the sugar into a bowl and dissolve with the water and lemon juice. Mix well.

◆ Add the whipped cream and stir together using a mixing spell.

◆ Pour the mixture into the molds and keep in the freezer overnight.

Professor Trelawney's Divination Tea

INGREDIENTS

serves 4

17 fluid ounces (½ l) spring water collected when the tawny owls are singing

For the following ingredients, see the chapter on Shopping:

Pinch of lemongrass picked while insects are humming

1 tablespoon dog rose leaves cut at daybreak

1 tablespoon elderberry flowers picked on the summer solstice

Pinch of candied orange peels prepared by moonlight

2 teaspoons sugar

If you think you see a Grim, consult a Seer immediately!

Preparation Time • 5 minutes • *Cooking Time* • 5 minutes

◆ Boil the spring water in a standard model cauldron.

◆ Four minutes after the first bubbles appear, remove the cauldron from the flame and throw in the remaining ingredients in the following order: lemongrass, dog rose leaves, elderberry flowers, and candied orange peels.

◆ Stir the mixture with your wand (or a spoon) and brew for 10 minutes.

◆ Pour into cups and sweeten with sugar as desired.

◆ Drink your tea and then, holding your cup in your left hand, stir the flowers, leaves, and peels counterclockwise three times.

◆ Now open your third eye and your divination manual and attempt to penetrate the veil of the future.

Professor Lupin's Chocolate Bonbons

INGREDIENTS

serves 6

7 ounces (200 g) baking chocolate

3½ ounces (100 g) butter

3½ ounces (100 g) powdered sugar

1 egg

1¾ ounces (50 g) ground hazelnuts

Indispensable in the event of a Dementor attack!

Preparation Time • **10** minutes + **15** minutes of resting time

◆ Place a large cauldron full of water over low heat.

◆ With the help of a crushing spell, break the chocolate into large pieces, then cut the butter into cubes. Pour the chocolate and butter into a small cauldron that you will place on top of the larger one so the heat of the water can gently melt the butter and chocolate together. Stir regularly with your wand (or a spoon).

◆ When the mixture is completely melted and warm, pour it into a dish and add the sugar and the egg. Combine and allow to cool for 15 minutes in a very cold place to allow the mixture to harden.

◆ Prepare two plates: one for the ground hazelnuts and the other to hold the bonbons.

◆ Use a small spoon to form walnut-size balls of the mixture. Roll the balls in the ground hazelnuts and place them on the second plate.

◆ These bonbons can be kept for 3 days in the refrigerator (a sort of ice chest used by non-magical people that runs on electricity).

UNOFFICIAL RECIPES INSPIRED BY

THE POTIONS MASTER

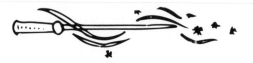

Bezoars

EQUIPMENT

1 rectangular mold around 11 x 7 inches (28 x 18 cm)

Parchment paper

1 dampened paintbrush

Dragon-hide gloves

INGREDIENTS

makes 15 stones

INGREDIENTS FOR WIZARDS

Mermaid scale powder

Dragon marrow

Full moon ray

Fairy fountain water

Powdered Bicorn horn

INGREDIENTS FOR NON-MAGICAL PEOPLE

6⅓ ounces (180 g) sugar

3 tablespoons molasses (see section on Shopping)

2 teaspoons honey

2 fluid ounces (60 ml) water

1 teaspoon baking soda

Effect:
Acts as an antidote to most potions.

Preparation Time • 20 minutes • *Cooking Time* • 20 minutes
Resting time • 1 hour and 30 minutes

◆ Mix together the mermaid scale powder (sugar), the dragon marrow (molasses), the moon ray (honey), and the water in a wide large model cauldron set over a low flame.

◆ Stir *without bring to a boil* until the mermaid scale powder (sugar) is completely dissolved.

◆ Dampen your paintbrush with a gentle hydration charm and draw it along the sides of your cauldron to remove any crystals that may have formed, then bring the mixture to a boil. When bubbles appear, let simmer for 7 minutes, not stirring, until the mixture takes on a pale caramel color.

◆ Put on your dragon-hide gloves and remove the cauldron from the fire.

◆ Pour in the powdered bicorn horn (baking soda) and stir until the mixture begins to froth and doubles in volume.

◆ Line your mold with parchment paper, carefully pour in your caramel mixture, and let rest for 1 hour 30 minutes until it has hardened.

◆ Remove from the mold and cut in pieces.

PROCLAMATION

Educational Decree
NO. 15-18

The Ministry would like to remind everyone of the following:

Potions and antidotes must be kept chilled and should be used in the hours following their preparation.

Only antidotes produced by wizards and witches with extensive experience should be considered sufficiently reliable.

In the event of a problem, call for help!

Elixir of Life

EQUIPMENT
1 pipette (see section on Techniques for Non-Magical People)

1 slotted spoon

1 colander

INGREDIENTS
makes 1 vial of 17 fluid ounces (500 ml)

INGREDIENTS FOR WIZARDS
Ubull juice

Venus herb leaves

1 swamp celery branch

Bacchus umbel seeds

Water from the Fountain of Youth

Sorcerer's Stone extract

INGREDIENTS FOR NON-MAGICAL PEOPLE
1 glass of neutral-flavored oil

13.5 fluid ounces (20 cl) water

$^1/_{10}$ ounce (2 g) agar-agar

2 spoonfuls fresh basil leaves

1 celery stalk

1 tablespoon lemon verbena leaves

1 spoonful fennel seeds (see section on Shopping)

$10^1/_{10}$ fluid ounces (30 cl) apple juice

Effect:
Ensures eternal life for as long as one drinks it.

Side Effects:
Indifference to major historical events.

Preparation Time · 20 minutes + 15 minutes of resting time

◆ Pour the oil into a jar with a wide neck and refrigerate.

◆ Bring 6¾ fluid ounces of water and the agar-agar to a boil in a small cauldron. When the first bubbles appear, remove from heat and add the fresh basil leaves. Brew for 15 minutes then remove the basil leaves.

◆ Using your pipette, transfer the basil juice one drop at a time into the container of cold oil. Collect the spheres with a Levitation spell (or a slotted spoon) and rinse them carefully in the colander.

◆ Pour the rest of the water from the Fountain of Youth into a standard model cauldron and place over medium heat.

◆ While the water is heating, rinse the swamp celery (or regular celery), the Venus herb leaves (verbena), and the Bacchus umbel seeds (fennel) and let them infuse the water for around 15 minutes without letting it boil, stirring in the direction of the sun's path.

◆ Let cool completely and, if the Sorcerer's Stone is not available, add the Spheres of Eternity created at the beginning of this recipe.

◆ Drink as needed.

Aging Potion

INGREDIENTS

makes 1 vial of 17 fluid ounces (500 ml)

INGREDIENTS FOR WIZARDS

Vélania leaves

Sitronensis concentrate

Sysimbre juice

Rutacé extract

Horned bulbilles

INGREDIENTS FOR NON-MAGICAL PEOPLE

6¾ fluid ounces (20 cl) jasmine tea

Juice of 1 lemon

Pineapple cubes

1⅔ fluid ounces (5 cl) orange syrup

5 fluid ounces (15 cl) lemon soda

Effect:

Gives the drinker the physical appearance of aging to greater or lesser degrees, depending upon how much is consumed.

Side Effects:

Growth of a beard that can reach 4 yards in length.

Preparation Time • 10 minutes

◆ Steep the vélania leaves (jasmine tea) in a small cauldron, then strain the liquid.

◆ Roll the rutacé (lemon) under your palm six times and cut it in half to juice it. Using sharp swipes of your wand, slice the horned bulbilles (pineapple) into cubes.

◆ Mix in the remaining ingredients in the order of the runic alphabet and chill.

Pepperup Potion

INGREDIENTS
for 1 vial of 17 fluid ounces (500 ml)

INGREDIENTS FOR WIZARDS

Dragon stone juice

Ridouble berry juice

Elettaria pod

Eight-point root

Yellow amada root

Salagama peel

Amber apple seed

Bearded tricorn powder

INGREDIENTS FOR NON-MAGICAL PEOPLE

1 cardamom pod

Pinch of ground ginger

2 tablespoons brown sugar

8½ fluid ounces (25 cl) black currant juice

8½ fluid ounces (25 cl) grape juice

1 star anise, whole

1 cinnamon stick

1 clove

Effect:
Cures head colds and chills.

Side Effects:
Causes steam to come out of the drinker's ears for several hours.

Preparation Time • 20 minutes + 15 minutes of resting time

◆ Press the dragon stones until you have extracted all of their juice.

◆ Crush the elettaria pod (cardamom), grind the yellow amada root (ginger) into a powder, and sift the bearded tricorn powder (brown sugar) to make it even lighter.

◆ Place a small cauldron over low heat and pour in the dragon stone juice (black currant) and the ridouble berry juice (grape).

◆ Add the remaining ingredients in this order: bearded tricorn powder (brown sugar), yellow amada (ginger), elletaria pod (cardamom), eight-point root (star anise), salagama peel (cinnamon), and the amber apple seed (clove).

◆ Stir until the bearded tricorn powder (brown sugar) is dissolved.

◆ Simmer for 15 minutes over low heat, then remove from heat and brew for another 15 minutes before filtering the liquid.

◆ To be consumed whenever you feel a cold coming on.

Wolfsbane Potion

INGREDIENTS
makes 1 vial of 17 fluid ounces (500 ml)

INGREDIENTS FOR WIZARDS

Unicorn milk

Massepinette powder

Arthemisia leaves

Full moon ray

INGREDIENTS FOR NON-MAGICAL PEOPLE

17 fluid ounces (50 cl) milk

1 ounce (30 g) ground almonds

1 spoonful chamomile leaves

$2^{4}/_{5}$ ounces (80 g) honey

Effect:
Eases discomfort related to the transformation of humans into werewolves.

Side Effects:
Heightened desire to take walks in the open air.

Preparation Time • **11** minutes

◆ Pour the unicorn milk into a standard model cauldron over a low flame.

◆ With a crumbling spell, grind the massepinettes (almonds) into a powder.

◆ When the milk is warm, add the arthemisia leaves (chamomile), then the ground almonds and the full moon ray (honey).

◆ Infuse for 10 minutes, stirring regularly: three times clockwise, twice counterclockwise, four times in the opposite direction, and once in the reverse direction (this step is essential), then remove the arthemisia leaves.

◆ To be consumed one week before the full moon.

Elixir to Induce Euphoria

INGREDIENTS
makes 1 vial of 17 fluid ounces (500 ml)

INGREDIENTS FOR
WIZARDS
Horned bulbilles

Sitronensis dilution

Yeti milk

Rutacé juice

Salagama peel

INGREDIENTS FOR NON-
MAGICAL PEOPLE
10$^{1}/_{10}$ fluid ounces (30 cl)
pineapple juice

5 fluid ounces (15 cl) coconut
milk

3$^{2}/_{5}$ fluid ounces (10 cl) orange
juice

Juice of 1 lemon

Pinch of ground cinnamon

Effect:
Puts drinker in an excellent mood.

Side Effects:
Strong tendency to sing and burst into laughter
for no particular reason (when this happens,
give the individual some mint).

Preparation Time • 10 minutes

◆ In a standard model cauldron, pour in the horned bulbilles
(pineapples) and the yeti milk (coconut milk) at the same time
and at the same speed.

◆ Stir for 3 minutes 33 seconds with a mixing spell.

◆ Next add the sitronensis dilution (orange) and the rutacé juice
(lemon) in the same fashion.

◆ Mix again for 3 minutes 33 seconds.

◆ Sprinkle with powdered salagama peel (cinnamon) and mix one
last time, blinking three times.

Polyjuice Potion

INGREDIENTS
makes 1 vial of 17 fluid ounces (500 ml)

INGREDIENTS FOR WIZARDS

Brassica trickster cabbage

Ubull mush

Unicorn milk

Rutacé bulbs

Bicorn horn powder

Fairy fountain water

Piece of the individual's body
(hair, toenail clippings)

INGREDIENTS FOR NON-MAGICAL PEOPLE

Half a red cabbage

²/₃ fluid ounce (2 cl) lemon juice

Spring water

Pinch of baking soda

6¾ fluid ounces (20 cl) milk

6¾ fluid ounces (20 cl)
applesauce

Piece of the individual's body
(hair, fingernail, etc.)

Effect:
Gives the drinker the appearance of another person
for one hour.

(Warning: only works on humans)

Side Effects:
Slight confusion caused by the changing of one's body.

Preparation Time • **15 minutes**

◆ Harvest a Brassica trickster cabbage that is fully mature (careful not to let yourself be tickled by its leaves; you will be unable to stop laughing for an entire day and night).

◆ Cut the cabbage into quarters, separate the leaves, and plunge them into a cauldron of water.

◆ Heat the water without letting it boil and brew for 15 minutes.

◆ Strain the leaves and collect the juice, observing its magnificent color.

◆ Gather the rutacé juice (lemon) and fairy fountain water and grind the bicorn horn (baking soda) until you have a very fine powder.

◆ The use of these ingredients will vary depending on the person whose appearance one desires to take on:

> To pass for someone younger than you, add the fairy fountain water (water).

> For a person the same age as you, pour in the unicorn milk (milk). (The unicorn milk must be given willingly in order to be used.)

> For someone older than you, finish it off with the rutacé juice (lemon).

> For a person who is the opposite gender, add the bicorn horn powder (baking soda). Be careful, for while it does not present any particular danger, the flavor is nevertheless quite peculiar.

◆ Next mix in the ubull mush (applesauce). Your potion should now have a muddy texture. Add the piece of the individual's body as well as a little water if needed and drink.

Strengthening Solution

INGREDIENTS
makes 1 vial of 17 fluid ounces (500 ml)

INGREDIENTS FOR WIZARDS
Lythrace juice

Ubull fruits

Phoenix tears

Melipone pod

INGREDIENTS FOR NON-MAGICAL PEOPLE
1 vanilla bean

3²/₅ fluid ounces (10 cl) applesauce

2 tablespoons maple syrup

13½ fluid ounces (40 cl) pomegranate juice

Effect:
Increases the power of the person who drinks it.

Side Effects:
Distinct penchant for wanting to beat all possible records for 1 day, 1 hour, and 1 minute.

Preparation Time • 10 minutes

◆ Rinse the ubull fruits (apples), peel and slice it, remove the seeds and place the slices in a cauldron over medium heat with a little water until the fruits can be easily crushed.

◆ Cut the melipone pod (vanilla) in half lengthwise, then use your wand (or the back of a knife) to scrape the inside of the bean in order to collect the seeds.

◆ Add the melipone seeds (vanilla) to the ubull compote (applesauce).

◆ Place the phoenix tears (maple syrup) in a standard model cauldron, add the ubull compote (applesauce), and pour in the lythrace juice (pomegranate).

◆ Stir three times in the direction a clock goes when turning back time, then four times in the opposite direction.

◆ Drink.

Liquid Luck

INGREDIENTS
makes 1 vial of 17 fluid ounces (500 ml)

INGREDIENTS FOR WIZARDS
Ubull juice

Full moon ray

Rutacé juice

Salamaga peel

Branch of musky faribola

INGREDIENTS FOR NON-MAGICAL PEOPLE
13½ fluid ounces (40 cl) apple juice

1 small sprig of thyme

1 cinnamon stick

Juice of 1 lemon

1 tablespoon white honey

Effect:

Renders every action undertaken for the duration of the potion successful.

Side Effects:

Excessive self-confidence.

Preparation Time • 10 minutes

◆ Gently heat the ubull juice (apple) over low heat in a standard model cauldron.

◆ Strip the branch of musky faribola (thyme) and sprinkle in the leaves with your left hand.

◆ Next add the salamaga peel (cinnamon), the rutacé juice (lemon), and the full moon ray (honey).

◆ Stir, making a "figure-eight" shape with your wand, until the full moon ray (honey) is completely melted.

◆ Simmer for 5 minutes and strain.

◆ Your potion should be a luminous golden color.

Love Potion

INGREDIENTS
makes 1 vial of 17 fluid ounces (500 ml)

INGREDIENTS FOR WIZARDS
Venus kiss extract
Cupid laughter bulbs
Sysimbre juice

INGREDIENTS FOR NON-MAGICAL PEOPLE
6¾ fluid ounces (20 cl) lychee juice

3²/₅ fluid ounces (10 cl) raspberry syrup

10¹/₁₀ fluid ounces (30 cl) lemon soda

Effect:
Gives the illusion of true love to whoever drinks it without ever, alas, actually producing it.

Side Effects:
Obsessive infatuation.

Note:
The scent of the potion is different for each person, depending on what attracts him or her the most.

Preparation Time • 10 minutes

◆ On the day of the week dedicated to Venus, and ideally on February 14th, extract the juice from the Cupid laughter bulbs (lychees).

◆ Hold your magic wand pointing toward your heart and prepare the potion as you recite a love poem, an ode of your own creation, or a romantic song.

◆ Pour the Venus kiss extract (raspberry) into a small cauldron, gently stir in the Cupid laughter juice, and lastly add the sysimbre juice (lemon soda).

◆ Your potion will turn a pearly color and will fill with tiny bubbles rising in a graceful spiral.

Truth Serum

INGREDIENTS
makes 1 vial of 17 fluid ounces (500 ml)

INGREDIENTS FOR WIZARDS
Water from Loch Ness

Rutacé juice

Mara elegancia berries

Sinople leaves

INGREDIENTS FOR NON-MAGICAL PEOPLE
1⅓ fluid ounces (40 ml) spring water

Juice of 1 lemon

3 strawberries

1 bunch of fresh mint

Effect:

Forces the person who ingests the elixir to reveal all of his or her secrets.

Side Effects:

Excessive honesty until the potion has completely worn off.

Preparation Time • 21 minutes + 30 minutes of resting time

◆ Select only the purest sinople leaves when harvesting near a unicorn's favorite sleeping place.

◆ After filtering the water from Loch Ness, heat it for 5 minutes 55 seconds.

◆ While the water heats, extract the rutacé juice (lemon) and cut the mara elegancia berries (strawberries) in quarters.

◆ Plunge the mara elegancia pieces (strawberries) and the rubbed sinople leaves (mint) into the cauldron, stir three times clockwise, and add the rutacé juice.

◆ Brew for 15 minutes then chill for 30 minutes and strain.

◆ The potion should be colorless, odorless, and have a totally irresistible flavor.

Forgetfulness Potion

INGREDIENTS
makes 1 vial of 17 fluid ounces (500 ml)

INGREDIENTS FOR WIZARDS
Rubeculia berries

Galande sap

1 sitronensis fruit

Water from the River Lethe

INGREDIENTS FOR NON-MAGICAL PEOPLE
3²/₅ fluid ounces (10 cl) black currant syrup

Spring water

6¾ fluid ounces (20 cl) orange juice

5 fluid ounces (15 cl) peach juice

Effect:
Provokes memory loss in the person who drinks it.

Side Effects:
The quantity and significance of what is forgotten as well as the duration of the amnesia depends on the quality of the potion.

Preparation Time • 10 minutes + 30 minutes of resting time

◆ Equip yourself with a standard model cauldron and place it over a low flame.

◆ Pour the rubeculia berries into the cauldron, cover with water from the River Lethe, and simmer until they release all of their juice. Then strain to collect the juice.

◆ Press down firmly on the sitronensis fruit and roll it seven times under your palm before cutting it in half to extract the juice.

◆ Pour the extract from the rubeculia berries (black currant syrup) into a vial.

◆ Using a Four-Point spell, determine which direction is north and pour 2 tablespoons of water from the River Lethe down the western side of the vial.

◆ Continue by adding the sitronensis juice (orange) down the northern side, then 2 more tablespoons of water down the eastern side and end by pouring the galande sap (peach) down the southern side.

Beautification Potion

INGREDIENTS
makes 1 vial of 17 fluid ounces (500 ml)

INGREDIENTS FOR WIZARDS
Pastinaca roots

Ubull juice

Salagama peel

Snow White powder

INGREDIENTS FOR NON-MAGICAL PEOPLE
13½ fluid ounces (40 cl) carrot juice

3⅖ fluid ounces (10 cl) apple juice

1 tablespoon ground hazelnuts

1 cinnamon stick

Effect:
Reveals on the exterior the internal beauty of whoever drinks the potion.

Side Effects:
Tendency to stare at oneself on any object with a reflective surface.

Preparation Time • 15 minutes   ◆   *Cooking Time* • 15 minutes

◆ Rinse and peel the pastinaca roots (carrots), cook them for 10 minutes in very hot water to extract their juice, then strain.

◆ In a small cauldron over a low flame, mix the pastinaca juice (carrot juice) with the ubull juice (apple juice).

◆ Gently stir with your left hand the same number of times as the day of your birth (three times if you were born on the third, etc.).

◆ When the mixture is warm, sprinkle the Snow White powder (ground hazelnuts) into the cauldron, add the salagama peel (cinnamon) and brew for 15 minutes before removing the peel.

◆ This potion can be consumed hot or cold.

Wit-Sharpening Potion

INGREDIENTS
makes 1 vial of 17 fluid ounces (500 ml)

INGREDIENTS FOR WIZARDS
Sphinx tears

Green rutacé juice

King grass leaves

Bicorn horn

INGREDIENTS FOR NON-MAGICAL PEOPLE
Pinch of baking soda

⅔ fluid ounce (2 cl) lime juice

13½ fluid ounces (40 cl) tomato juice

Pinch of basil leaves

Effect:
Effects greater concentration.

Side Effects:
Strong tendency to want to solve any and all riddles one encounters.

Preparation Time • 10 minutes

◆ In order to put yourself in the concentrated mindset necessary to make this potion, recite your alphabet backwards.

◆ Grind the bicorn horn (baking soda) into a very fine powder.

◆ Place the green rutacé juice (lime) in a small cauldron then sprinkle with bicorn horn powder (baking soda).

◆ Observe the reaction: the mixture should whistle, crackle, and foam.

◆ Add the sphinx tears (tomato juice) little by little to dilute the mixture.

◆ Next add the king grass leaves (basil), continuing to recite the alphabet.

◆ Brew for 5 minutes and taste not once but twice.

Babbling Beverage

EQUIPMENT
1 pipette

1 long spoon

INGREDIENTS
makes 1 vial of 17 fluid ounces (500 ml)

INGREDIENTS FOR WIZARDS
Babilleurs barbus extract

Ubull juice

Galande sap

Sitronensis decoction

Farfadet's tears of laughter

INGREDIENTS FOR NON-MAGICAL PEOPLE
3²/₅ fluid ounces (10 cl) cherry syrup

1²/₃ fluid ounces (5 cl) orange juice

3²/₅ fluid ounces (10 cl) apple juice

3²/₅ fluid ounces (10 cl) peach juice

5 fluid ounces (15 cl) sports drink (blue)

Effect:
Causes the person who drinks it to continually yammer on, spewing nonsense and saying things that no one can make heads or tails of.

Side Effects:
Duration of effect depends on the quantity consumed.

Warning:
Should not be ingested the same day as an Elixir to Induce Euphoria. The recipient risks causing intense aggravation to those around him or her.

Preparation Time • 5 minutes

◆ Measure the liquid quantities with extreme precision.

◆ Pour the babilleurs barbus syrup (cherry) into a standard model cauldron.

◆ Using your pipette, transfer the sitronensis decoction (orange) to the cauldron, letting it trickle down the length of a spoon, in order to keep the ingredients from mixing.

◆ Proceed in the same fashion for the ubull juice (apple), the garande sap (peach), and the Farfadet's tears of laughter (blue drink).

◆ The potion's bright colors should remain very distinct until the moment it is consumed. After one sip, the mixture takes on a color described as that of a "shimmering toad."

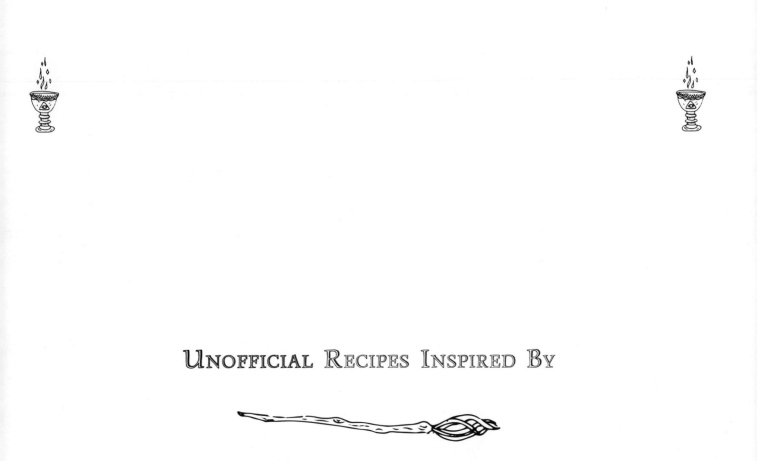

UNOFFICIAL RECIPES INSPIRED BY

THE KNIGHT BUS

Stan's Specialty

INGREDIENTS

serves 4

34 fluid ounces (1 l) milk

5⅓ ounces (150 g) dark chocolate

1 vanilla bean

4 tablespoons sugar

1 cinnamon stick

1 teaspoon ground ginger

Keep a good hold of your mug—
The Knight Bus guarantees a bumpy ride!

Preparation and Cooking Time • 20 minutes

◆ Pour the milk into a cauldron suitable for traveling on the Knight Bus.

◆ Heat over a very low flame to keep any milk from evaporating (and to keep its whistling sound from terrifying other passengers).

◆ Using a crushing spell, break the chocolate into pieces and add to the milk.

◆ Allow the chocolate to melt gently in order to avoid splatters on the floor of the bus.

◆ Slice the vanilla bean lengthwise. (The Gouging spell is a bad idea—if the bus suddenly goes over a bump this could make holes in the curtains).

◆ Scrape the bean to collect the seeds, then add the bean and seeds to the cauldron.

◆ When the chocolate is melted, add the sugar, cinnamon, and ginger. Simmer for 10 minutes, stirring gently. Remove the vanilla beans and the cinnamon stick and pour into mugs. (Do not use the Levitation charm when the bus slows down. The driver still hasn't gotten over the last time . . .)

UNOFFICIAL RECIPES INSPIRED BY

FLOREAN FORTESCUE'S ICE CREAM PARLOUR

Gryffindor House Cup

EQUIPMENT
1 piping bag (see Techniques for Non-Magical People)

Parchment paper

INGREDIENTS
serves 4

3½ ounces (100 g) apricot ice cream

3½ ounces (100 g) strawberry ice cream

2¹⁄₁₀ ounces (60 g) crushed hazelnuts

1 tablespoon sugar

The house of courage and chivalry!

Preparation and Cooking Time • 10 minutes

◆ Take the ice creams out of the freezer.

◆ Pour the hazelnuts into a pan over high heat with the sugar.

◆ Use a dragon-breath spell or let the nuts caramelize for a few minutes, stirring constantly, until they are golden brown.

◆ Place the parchment paper vertically inside the piping bag to form a partition between two separate compartments.

◆ Pour the first ice cream into one compartment and the second ice cream into the other.

◆ Remove the sheet of parchment paper and gently pipe pretty and colorful spirals into your serving cups.

◆ Sprinkle with caramelized hazelnuts and serve without waiting another moment.

Hufflepuff House Cup

EQUIPMENT

1 piping bag (see Techniques for Non-Magical People)

Parchment paper

INGREDIENTS

serves 4

3½ ounces (100 g) pear ice cream

3½ ounces (100 g) chocolate ice cream

2¹/₁₀ ounces (60 g) diced hazelnut praline

The house of loyalty and hard work!

Preparation Time • 5 minutes

◆ Take the ice creams out of the freezer.

◆ Place the parchment paper vertically inside the piping bag to form a partition between two separate compartments.

◆ Pour the first ice cream into one compartment and the second ice cream into the other.

◆ Remove the sheet of parchment paper and gently pipe pretty and colorful spirals into your serving cups.

◆ With a wave of your wand, divide the diced praline between the cups and serve immediately.

Ravenclaw House Cup

EQUIPMENT
1 piping bag (see Techniques for Non-Magical People)

Parchment paper

INGREDIENTS
serves 4

3½ ounces (100 g) blackberry ice cream

3½ ounces (100 g) vanilla ice cream

2¹⁄₁₀ ounces (60 g) marshmallows

The house of knowledge and wit!

Preparation and Cooking Time • **10 minutes**

◆ Take the ice cream out of the freezer.

◆ Place the parchment paper vertically inside the piping bag to form a partition between two separate compartments.

◆ Pour the first ice cream into one compartment and the second ice cream into the other.

◆ Remove the sheet of parchment paper and gently pipe pretty and colorful spirals into your serving cups.

◆ Sprinkle with small pieces of marshmallow and serve promptly.

Slytherin House Cup

EQUIPMENT

1 piping bag (see Techniques for Non-Magical People)

Parchment paper

INGREDIENTS

serves 4

3½ ounces (100 g) mint ice cream

3½ ounces (100 g) white chocolate ice cream

2¹⁄₁₀ ounces (60 g) mini meringues

The house of ambition and cunning!

Preparation Time • 5 minutes

◆ Take the ice creams out of the freezer.

◆ Place the parchment paper vertically inside the piping bag to form a partition between two separate compartments.

◆ Pour the first ice cream into one compartment and the second ice cream into the other.

◆ Remove the sheet of parchment paper using a Levitation charm and gently pipe pretty and colorful spirals into your serving cups.

◆ Sprinkle with mini meringues and serve right away.

Florean's Special

You'll keep coming back for more!

EQUIPMENT

1 piping bag (see Techniques for Non-Magical People)

Parchment paper

INGREDIENTS

serves 4

3½ ounces (100 g) strawberry ice cream

3½ ounces (100 g) milk chocolate ice cream

2¹/₁₀ ounces (60 g) softened peanut butter

Preparation Time • 10 minutes

◆ Take the ice creams out of the freezer.

◆ Place the parchment paper vertically inside the piping bag to form a partition between two separate compartments.

◆ With a languid sweep of your wand, pour the first ice cream into one compartment and the second ice cream into the other.

◆ Remove the sheet of parchment paper and gently pipe pretty and colorful spirals into your serving cups.

◆ Drizzle softened peanut butter generously over each cup and serve as soon as you can.

Centaur's Temperament

EQUIPMENT

Ice cream scoop

Cups or bowls of your choice

INGREDIENTS

serves 4

3½ ounces (100 g) dark
    chocolate ice cream

3½ ounces (100 g) milk
    chocolate ice cream

2¹⁄₁₀ ounces (60 g) pecans

1 tablespoon sugar

Ice cream cones

Mighty and Mysterious

Preparation and Cooking Time • 10 minutes

◆ Take the ice creams out of the freezer and roughly chop the nuts.

◆ Add the nuts and sugar to a pan over high heat. Let the nuts caramelize for a few minutes and stir constantly until the nuts are light brown.

◆ Using a scooping spell (or an ice cream scoop), place perfect dollops of ice cream in your cones, alternating flavors as you wish.

◆ Sprinkle with caramelized pecans and serve without delay.

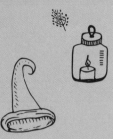

Fairy Kiss

EQUIPMENT
1 piping bag (see Techniques for Non-Magical People)

Parchment paper

INGREDIENTS
serves 4

3½ ounces (100 g) passion fruit ice cream

3½ ounces (100 g) milk chocolate ice cream

2¹⁄₁₀ ounces (60 g) pink biscuits of Reims

Will you be able to resist it?

Preparation Time • 5 minutes

◆ Take the ice creams out of the freezer.

◆ Perform a crushing spell to crumble the biscuits into pieces.

◆ Place the parchment paper vertically inside the piping bag to form a partition between two separate compartments.

◆ Pour the first ice cream into one compartment and the second ice cream into the other.

◆ Remove the sheet of parchment paper using a Levitation charm and gently pipe pretty and colorful spirals into your serving cups.

◆ Sprinkle with pink biscuit pieces and serve at once.

Goblin Humor

EQUIPMENT
I piping bag (see Techniques for Non-Magical People)

Parchment paper

INGREDIENTS
serves 4

3½ ounces (100 g) praline ice cream

3½ ounces (100 g) mixed berry ice cream

2¹/₁₀ ounces (60 g) unsalted pistachios

A well-kept secret!

Preparation and Cooking Time • 5 minutes

◆ Take the ice creams out of the freezer.

◆ Using a crushing spell, break the pistachios into pieces.

◆ Place the parchment paper vertically inside the piping bag to form a partition between two separate compartments.

◆ Pour the first ice cream into one compartment and the second ice cream into the other.

◆ Remove the sheet of parchment paper and gently pipe pretty and colorful spirals into your serving cups.

◆ Sprinkle with pistachio pieces and serve at any moment.

Floo Powder Ice Cream

EQUIPMENT

1 piping bag (see Techniques for Non-Magical People)

Parchment paper

INGREDIENTS

serves 4

3½ ounces (100 g) coffee ice cream

3½ ounces (100 g) caramel ice cream

2¹⁄₁₀ ounces (60 g) slivered almonds

1 tablespoon sugar

A treat that will take you on a trip!

Preparation and Cooking Time • 10 minutes

◆ Take the ice creams out of the freezer.

◆ Add the slivered almonds and sugar to a pan over high heat. Allow the nuts to caramelize, stirring constantly until the almonds are golden brown.

◆ Place the parchment paper vertically inside the piping bag to form a partition between two separate compartments, or use a splitting charm.

◆ Pour the first ice cream into one compartment and the second ice cream into the other.

◆ Remove the sheet of parchment paper and gently pipe pretty and colorful spirals into your serving cups.

◆ Sprinkle with caramelized almonds and serve without further ado.

Fang's Nap

A marvelous dream.

EQUIPMENT

1 piping bag (see Techniques for
Non-Magical People)

Parchment paper

INGREDIENTS

serves 4

3½ ounces (100 g) speculoos
ice cream (cinnamon or
gingerbread ice cream can also
be used)

3½ ounces (100 g) fig ice cream

2¹⁄₁₀ ounces (60 g) walnuts

1 tablespoon sugar

Preparation and Cooking Time • **10** minutes

◆ Take the ice creams out of the freezer.

◆ Using a crushing spell, break the walnuts into pieces then place them in a pan over high heat along with the sugar. Allow the nuts to caramelize, stirring constantly until they have turned golden brown.

◆ Place the parchment paper vertically inside the piping bag to form a partition between two separate compartments.

◆ Pour the first ice cream into one compartment and the second ice cream into the other.

◆ Remove the sheet of parchment paper and gently pipe pretty and colorful spirals into your serving cups.

◆ Sprinkle with caramelized walnut pieces and serve quickly.

Dragon Smile

An experience you won't soon forget!

EQUIPMENT

1 piping bag (see Techniques for Non-Magical People)

Parchment paper

INGREDIENTS

serves 4

3½ ounces (100 g) pistachio ice cream

3½ ounces (100 g) cherry ice cream

2¹⁄₁₀ ounces (60 g) nougat

Preparation and Cooking Time • 5 minutes

◆ Take the ice creams out of the freezer.

◆ With sharp swipes of your wand, cut the nougat into ⅓ inch (1 cm) cubes.

◆ Place the parchment paper vertically inside the piping bag to form a partition between two separate compartments.

◆ Pour the first ice cream into one compartment and the second ice cream into the other.

◆ Remove the sheet of parchment paper and gently pipe pretty and colorful spirals into your serving cups.

◆ Sprinkle with nougat pieces and serve post-haste.

Unicorn Dream

EQUIPMENT

1 piping bag (see Techniques for
Non-Magical People)

Parchment paper

INGREDIENTS

serves 4

3½ ounces (100 g) vanilla ice
cream

3½ ounces (100 g) honey ice
cream

2¹/₁₀ ounces (60 g) rolled oats (or
plain corn flakes)

An enchanting tenderness.

Preparation and Cooking Time • 5 minutes

◆ Take the ice creams out of the freezer.

◆ Use a dragon-breath spell to toast the rolled oats (but not the
corn flakes) for a few minutes in a pan over high heat.

◆ Place the parchment paper vertically inside the piping bag to
form a partition between two separate compartments.

◆ Pour the first ice cream into one compartment and the second
ice cream into the other.

◆ Remove the sheet of parchment paper and gently pipe pretty
and colorful spirals into your serving cups.

◆ Sprinkle with lightly toasted rolled oats and serve before too
much time goes by.

Phoenix Song

EQUIPMENT
Ice cream scoop
Cups or bowls of your choice

INGREDIENTS
serves 4
3½ ounces (100 g) mango ice cream
3½ ounces (100 g) pineapple ice cream
3½ ounces (100 g) fresh raspberries

So delicious it will bring tears to your eyes.

Preparation Time • 5 minutes

◆ Take the ice creams out of the freezer.

◆ Rinse the raspberries using a hydration charm.

◆ Using a scooping spell (or an ice cream scoop), place perfect dollops of ice cream in a cup or bowl of your choice, alternating flavors as you wish.

◆ Sprinkle with raspberries and serve right away.

Butterbeer Ice Cream

EQUIPMENT

1 piping bag (see Techniques for Non-Magical People)

Parchment paper

INGREDIENTS

serves 4

3½ ounces (100 g) vanilla ice cream

3½ ounces (100 g) whipped cream

2 fluid ounces (60 ml) butterscotch syrup (see Shopping)

2¹⁄₁₀ ounces (60 g) chopped hazelnuts

A success since 1588!

Preparation and Cooking Time • 5 minutes

◆ Transfer the ice cream to your piping bag and gently pipe pretty spirals into your serving cups.

◆ With an unwavering whirl of your wand, cover the ice cream with whipped cream, then, with a gentle flick of your wand, drizzle the syrup over it.

◆ Sprinkle with hazelnuts and serve very soon.

Auror's Fancy

EQUIPMENT
Ice cream scoop
Cups or bowls of your choice

INGREDIENTS
serves 4
2$\frac{1}{10}$ ounces (60 g) popcorn
  kernels

1 tablespoon sugar

3½ ounces (100 g) apple ice
  cream

3½ ounces (100 g) caramel ice
  cream

A delicacy that even the forces of darkness cannot resist!

Preparation and Cooking Time • 10 minutes

◆ Pour the popcorn kernels into a pan over high heat and cover
with a lid.

◆ Cast an Exploding charm to cause the kernels to burst, then
sprinkle them with sugar and allow them to caramelize, stirring
constantly, until the popcorn is golden brown.

◆ Using a scooping spell (or an ice cream scoop), place perfect
portions of ice cream in your serving bowls, alternating flavors as
you wish.

◆ Sprinkle with caramelized popcorn and serve without
hesitation. (It is said that it was this recipe that got Florean into
trouble with the Death Eaters.)

UNOFFICIAL RECIPES INSPIRED BY

HONEYDUKE'S

Chocolate Frogs

EQUIPMENT

1 frog-shaped mold (see section
on Shopping)

INGREDIENTS

serves 6

1¾ ounces (50 g) milk chocolate

1¾ ounces (50 g) dark chocolate

2⅘ ounces (80 g) marshmallows

Preparation Time • 20 minutes + resting time: 2 hours and 2 x 30 min

◆ Break the chocolate into large pieces with a crushing spell.

◆ Fill a large model cauldron with clear water then place a smaller
cauldron over it, making sure that the water level is always high
enough to touch the base of the smaller cauldron. Pour the
chocolate pieces into the smaller cauldron and gently melt over
low heat.

◆ When the chocolate forms a smooth ribbon, pour it into the
frog molds, dividing it evenly using a Levitation charm, and
rotate molds over a sheet of parchment paper (or a plate) so that
any excess chocolate runs off, leaving just a thin coating.

◆ Chill the molds for 30 minutes.

◆ Gently melt the marshmallows with a little bit of water to obtain
a smooth cream.

◆ Take the frogs out of the refrigerator, fill the interior with
melted marshmallow, using a knife to smooth everything out, and
chill for at least 2 more hours (the longer your frogs have chilled,
the better they will be).

◆ Melt the rest of the chocolate again the same way you did earlier
and delicately coat the frogs, smoothing away any excess chocolate.
Chill for 30 minutes.

◆ Carefully remove the frogs from the molds and recite a fidget
spell to bring them to life.

Pumpkin Fizz Jellies

EQUIPMENT

1 pumpkin-shaped cookie cutter (see section on Techniques for Non-Magical People)

1 blender

1 small plate

1 large plate

INGREDIENTS

makes 18 ounces (500 g)

$8^4/_5$ ounces (250 g) pumpkin flesh (Cinderella pumpkin or peanut pumpkin varieties can also be used)

$11^1/_2$ ounces (325 g) jam sugar

Splash of lemon juice

Preparation Time • 20 minutes + resting time 2 hours
Cooking Time • 10 minutes

◆ Put on your dragon-hide gloves. Then, using a Severing charm, remove the pumpkin skin.

◆ Cut the pumpkin flesh into pieces and mix in the blender on high.

◆ Add the pumpkin, sugar, and lemon juice to a medium size cauldron and bring to a boil.

◆ Place a small plate in the freezer or cast a Freezing charm on it.

◆ Stir constantly while singing until all of the sugar has dissolved (essential for the success of this recipe).

◆ After 10 minutes of cooking, remove the plate from the freezer and pour a few drops of the mixture onto it. Count to ten and hold the plate vertically. Your jelly candy is perfect if it remains in place. If the syrup runs, continue cooking and perform the test again.

◆ Line the large plate with parchment paper, letting some hang over the edge, then pour the mixture onto the plate and let it cool for two hours.

◆ When the mixture is completely cooled, cut out the pumpkins using your cookie cutter and roll them in sugar so you can hold them without getting your fingers stuck.

Cauldron Cakes

Preparation Time • 30 minutes ♦ *Cooking Time* • 45 minutes

EQUIPMENT

1 muffin tray

1 piping bag (see section on Techniques for Non-Magical People)

Parchment paper

INGREDIENTS

serves 6

8⅘ ounces (250 g) baking chocolate

6⅓ ounces (180 g) butter

6 eggs

3½ ounces (100 g) flour

½ ounce (15 g) yeast

6⅓ ounces (180 g) sugar

3½ ounces (100 g) whipped cream

Rainbow sprinkles for decoration

♦ Break the chocolates into large pieces using a crushing spell. Set aside around one quarter of the chocolate and one walnut-sized piece for each guest.

♦ Fill a large model cauldron with clear water and place a smaller cauldron on top of it, making sure that the water level remains high enough to touch the base of the smaller cauldron. Add the chocolate pieces and the butter to the small cauldron and melt them gently over low heat.

♦ Crack the eggs and pour the whites into a bowl with a pinch of salt (set aside the yolks for a later step). Cast a frothing spell or use an electric beater and beat the egg whites into stiff peaks. The whites are ready when you can turn the bowl over your head without having a white and mousse-like hat suddenly fall on your head.

♦ Preheat your oven to 350°F (180°C, th. 6–7).

♦ Sift the flour, yeast, and sugar into a separate bowl. Next add the egg yolks and the butter-chocolate mixture. Use a mixing spell to stir gently until you have a cream with a uniform mousse-like texture.

♦ Now add the beaten egg whites, trying not to stir more than necessary in order to incorporate as much air into your batter as possible.

♦ Fill your muffin molds two thirds of the way, place one piece of un-melted chocolate inside the batter, and bake for 45 minutes.

♦ While the cakes bake, melt the rest of the chocolate the same way you did before. Transfer some of the chocolate to the piping bag (or a freezer storage bag with one corner cut off). Keep the rest of the chocolate warm.

♦ Draw cauldron handles on a sheet of parchment paper with your piping bag. Use a Freezing charm or chill for 30 minutes.

♦ Check to see if your cakes are baked: plunge the tip of your wand (or a knife) into the center. It should come out clean and dry.

(continued)

◆ Once the cakes have cooled, use a small spoon to hollow out the flat part of the cake.

◆ Dip the rounded part of the cake in melted chocolate to coat it completely. Let dry on a plate or cooling rack.

◆ "Fill" the hollowed cauldron with whipped cream, decorate with sprinkles, and attach the handles.

Licorice Wands

EQUIPMENT

I wand-shaped candy mold (see sections on Techniques for Non-Magical People and Shopping)

INGREDIENTS

serves 6

1¾ ounces (50 g) milk chocolate

1¾ ounces (50 g) dark chocolate

18 ounces (500 g) unsweetened condensed milk

3–4 pinches of agar-agar

I teaspoon per wand of: licorice wheels pieces, citrus peels, marshmallows cut in small rods, caramels, cubes of candied fruit, nuts (walnuts, hazelnuts, almonds, etc.), fruit jelly candies, etc.

Preparation Time • 20 minutes + resting time: 2 hours and 2 x 30 minutes

◆ Break the chocolates into large pieces with the help of a crushing spell.

◆ Fill a large model cauldron with clear water, then place a small cauldron on top of it, making sure that the water level remains high enough to touch the base of the smaller cauldron. Add the pieces of chocolate to the small cauldron and gently melt over low heat.

◆ When the chocolate resembles a smooth ribbon, remove three quarters of it (for the wand molds) and set the rest aside. With a sweep of your wand, carefully fill each mold and rotate them over a sheet of parchment paper (or a plate) to allow any excess chocolate to run off, leaving just a thin layer in the molds.

◆ Chill the molds for 30 minutes.

◆ While the chocolate cools, bring the condensed milk to a boil with a dragon-breath spell. As soon as bubbles appear, lower the heat and add the agar-agar. Stir and continue cooking for 5 minutes.

◆ Take out the chilled chocolate wands and fill them the rest of the way with condensed milk and candies of your choice. Smooth away any excess and chill for another 2 hours.

◆ Melt the rest of the chocolate the same way you did earlier, carefully coat the wands, smoothing away any excess chocolate, and chill for 30 minutes.

◆ Gently remove the wands from the molds and recite a spell of your choosing to see which wand is best for you.

◆ Don't forget: *It is always the wand that chooses the wizard.*

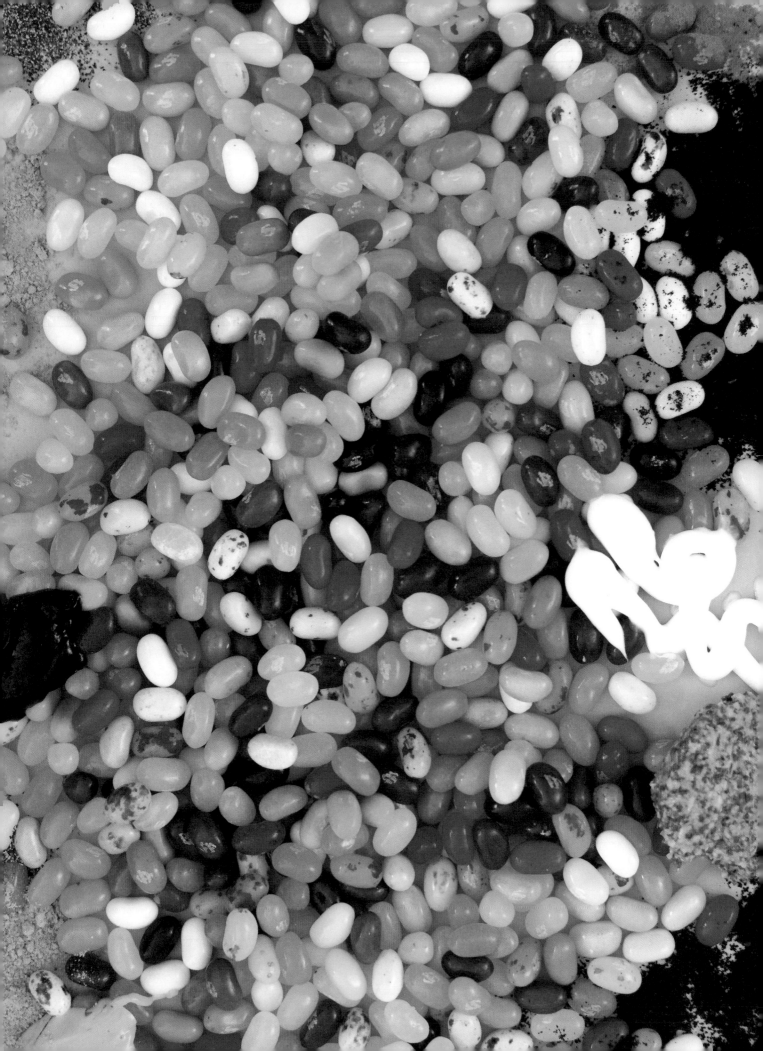

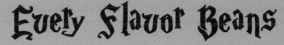

Every Flavor Beans

EQUIPMENT

1 very thin 5 ml syringe (without needle)

INGREDIENTS

serves 6

1 pack of jelly beans (any brand)

1 teaspoon (each) of:

Hazelnut spread (p. 5)

Coconut powder

Freeze-dried coffee

Banana purée

Orange jelly (p. 15)

Mint jelly

Strawberry jam

Toast ground into breadcrumbs

Blueberry jelly

Cherry preserves

Ground cinnamon

Curry paste

Freshly ground pepper

Spinach purée

Canned sardines, crushed

Mustard

Mixed sausages

White bean purée

Toothpaste

Preparation Time • 45 minutes

◆ Carefully make a cut in each jelly bean with the tip of a small knife.

◆ Use the syringe to transfer one half ml of an ingredient into a jelly bean. Place the tip of the syringe into the cut you have made and inject to fill the candy completely.

◆ Proceed in the same way for all of the every flavor beans. (Since this is a rather time-consuming task, it is advisable to obtain the help of several house-elves.)

◆ The every flavor beans can be refrigerated and should be eaten quickly.

Pink Coconut Ices

EQUIPMENT
1 large dish
Parchment paper

INGREDIENTS
makes 15 treats

8⁴/₅ ounces (250 g) powdered
    sugar

7 ounces (200 g) unsweetened
    condensed milk

1 pound (450 g) shredded
    coconut

Rainbow sprinkles for decoration

Preparation Time • 5 minutes + 2 hours resting time

◆ Use a mixing spell to stir the powdered sugar, condensed milk, and shredded coconut together until the mixture has a uniform consistency.

◆ Line the dish with parchment paper and cover with the coconut mixture, carefully smoothing it out before chilling for at least 2 hours.

◆ Now cut into cubes and roll in rainbow sprinkles.

◆ Keep refrigerated or cast a Freezing charm.

Cockroach Clusters

EQUIPMENT
6 mini tart pans (3 inches, or 7.5 cm—see section on Techniques for Non-Magical People)

INGREDIENTS
makes 6 nests and 6 cockroaches

For the nests:
7 ounces (200 g) baking chocolate

7 ounces (200 g) plain unsweetened corn flakes

1¾ ounces (50 g) candied fruit cubes

For the cockroaches:
3½ ounces (100 g) dates

1¾ ounces (50 g) nougat

Preparation Time • 20 minutes + resting time: 30 minutes

◆ Break the chocolate into large pieces with the help of a crushing spell.

◆ Fill a large model cauldron with clear water then place a smaller cauldron on top of it, making sure that the water level remains high enough to touch the base of the smaller cauldron. Add the chocolate pieces to the small cauldron and gently melt over low heat.

◆ With another crushing spell, crush the cornflakes in a bowl. Cut the candied fruit into small cubes and add to the bowl.

◆ When the chocolate forms a smooth ribbon, pour it into the bowl and blend with a mixing spell.

◆ Line the tart molds with microwave safe plastic wrap.

◆ Divide the chocolate between the pans and chill for 30 minutes.

◆ Remove from the tart pans once the chocolate has set and remove the plastic wrap.

◆ Using a Severing charm, slice open the dates and remove the pits with a Levitation charm. Slice the nougat into thin strips a bit longer than the dates, then stuff the nougat inside the dates, allowing the nougat to stick out at one end to form the cockroach head.

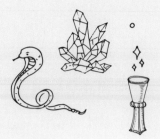
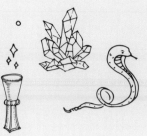

Stickyteeth Caramels

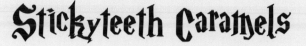

EQUIPMENT

1 star-shaped cookie cutter (see section on Techniques for Non-Magical People)

Parchment paper

1 dish

INGREDIENTS

makes 20 caramels

$2^{1}/_{10}$ ounces (60 g) butter

7 ounces (200 g) sweetened condensed milk

4 ounces (125 g) powdered sugar

1 tablespoon honey

Preparation Time • 30 minutes + 1 hour resting time

◆ In a small model cauldron, warm the butter, condensed milk, sugar, and honey over low heat.

◆ Line the dish with parchment paper, leaving some hanging over the edge.

◆ When the sugar has completely dissolved, lower the heat and cook for 20 minutes, stirring constantly and never allowing the mixture to boil. Boiling will cause the caramel to betray you by sticking to the bottom of the pot, and it might burn.

◆ As it cooks, the color of the mixture will go from white to golden brown and will thicken little by little to form a beautiful smooth and thick cream. If the caramel is too runny, continue cooking for a few more minutes.

◆ Put on your protective gloves and pour the caramel onto the dish in a layer $^{1}/_{3}$ inch (1 cm) thick. Smooth it out and chill for around 1 hour (or at least 30 minutes).

◆ When the caramel has set, cut it using sharp swipes of your wand, or your cookie cutter, and store in a cool place.

Chocoballs

INGREDIENTS

serves 6

7 ounces (200 g) baking
   chocolate

3½ ounces (100 g) butter

3½ ounces (100 g) powdered
   sugar

3½ ounces (100 g) unsweetened
   puffed rice

Chocolate sprinkles for
   decoration

Preparation Time • 20 minutes + resting time: 30 minutes

◆ Break the chocolate into large pieces with the help of a crushing spell.

◆ Fill a large model cauldron with clear water, then place a small cauldron on top of it, making sure that the water level remains high enough to touch the base of the small cauldron. Add the chocolate pieces and butter to the small cauldron and gently melt over low heat. When the mixture forms a smooth ribbon, pour it into a bowl and add the sugar and puffed rice.

◆ Combine with a mixing spell and chill for 30 minutes until the mixture is firm.

◆ Scoop out a spoonful of the mixture and roll it between your hands to form a small ball.

◆ Roll the chocoballs in chocolate sprinkles and keep refrigerated.

Jelly Slugs

◆ Rinse the apples and use your blender or a crumbling charm to purée them.

◆ Place a small plate in the freezer or cast a Freezing charm on it.

◆ Pour the apple purée, water, lemon juice, and mint leaves into a standard model cauldron and bring to a boil using a dragon-breath spell. Cook for 10 minutes then filter over a bowl to collect the juice.

◆ Weigh the juice and add an equal quantity of jam sugar.

◆ Transfer this mixture to the cauldron and boil for 4–7 minutes. The mixture is ready when a drop placed on the cold plate remains solid long enough for you to count to ten.

◆ Pour the jelly slug mixture into the molds and chill to set.

EQUIPMENT

1 mini madeleine pan (see section on Techniques for Non-Magical People)

1 blender

1 small plate

INGREDIENTS

makes 20 slugs

8⁴⁄₅ ounces (250 g) Granny Smith apples not treated with growth serum or No-Pest Spray

8½ fluid ounces (250 ml) water

1 fluid ounce (30 ml) lemon juice

6¹⁄₅ ounces (175 g) mint leaves from the Hogwarts garden

4²⁄₅ ounces (125 g) jam sugar (quantity will vary depending on amount of juice collected)

UNOFFICIAL RECIPES INSPIRED BY

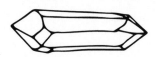

THE BURROW

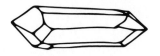

SANDWICHES

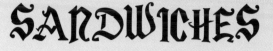

Assorted sandwiches: for voyages on the school train, afternoons of flying broomsticks, or a thorough cleaning of the Order of the Phoenix headquarters.

Ron's Usual

INGREDIENTS

makes 4 sandwiches

8 slices whole wheat bread

$8^4/_5$ ounces (250 g) green cabbage, thinly sliced

$2^1/_{10}$ ounces (60 g) thick crème fraîche

$2^1/_{10}$ ounces (60 g) traditional grain mustard

7 ounces (200 g) grated cheddar

7 ounces (200 g) corned beef

Unfortunately for Ron, Mrs. Weasley never remembers that her youngest son doesn't like corned beef.

Preparation Time • 5 minutes

◆ Using a dragon-breath spell, toast the slices of bread.

◆ Rinse the green cabbage and dry it carefully.

◆ In a small bowl, mix the crème fraîche and mustard.

◆ Spread this mixture generously on the slices of bread, then top one slice with cabbage and corned beef. Sprinkle with grated cheddar and top with a second slice of bread.

Fred and George's Merrymaking

INGREDIENTS

makes 4 sandwiches

8 slices rye bread

7 ounces (200 g) cheddar cheese
(or aged gouda)

8⁴/₅ ounces (250 g) smoked trout

I teaspoon paprika

2¹/₁₀ ounces (60 g) butter

Preparation Time • 5 minutes

◆ Cast a dragon-breath spell to toast the bread, then grate the cheddar with staccato flicks of your wand and slice the trout into strips using sharp swipes of your wand.

◆ Butter each slice of toasted bread and sprinkle with a pinch of paprika. Top with the grated cheddar and smoked trout and finish it off with the second slice of bread.

Percy's Darling

Ingredients

makes 4 sandwiches

1 bunch fresh mint

3½ ounces (100 g) cooked peas

3½ ounces (100 g) fromage blanc

7 ounces (200 g) canned tuna

8 slices white bread

Preparation Time • 5 minutes

◆ Rinse and finely chop the mint leaves.

◆ Crush the peas in a bowl or use a crumbling spell. Pour in the fromage blanc and beat vigorously to give the mixture volume.

◆ Break the tuna into chunks and add the chopped mint.

◆ Spread each slice of bread with the pea purée, sprinkle generously with the tuna and mint mixture, and delicately place the second slice of bread on top, making sure the edges are perfectly aligned.

Ginny's Favorite

INGREDIENTS
makes 4 sandwiches

8 slices white bread

7 ounces (200 g) bacon

7 ounces (200 g) sun-dried
  tomatoes

1 ball mozzarella cheese

4 tablespoons liquid honey

Preparation Time • 5 minutes   ◆   *Cooking Time* • 5 minutes

◆ Toast the bread until crisp and golden.

◆ In a pan, fry the bacon for 5 minutes then leave to dry with the sun-dried tomatoes on a paper towel.

◆ Slice the mozzarella into thin pieces, place a few on the first piece of toast, pour on half the honey, then add the tomatoes and bacon followed by the remaining honey and mozzarella. Top with a second slice of toast.

Charlie's Number One

INGREDIENTS

makes 4 sandwiches

8 slices country bread

7 ounces (200 g) roasted chicken

1 teaspoon curry powder

3½ ounces (100 g) fromage frais

1 ounce (30 g) slivered almonds

1 ounce (30 g) raisins

Preparation Time • 5 minutes

◆ Cast a dragon-breath spell to toast the bread.

◆ Cut the chicken into strips using sharp swipes of your wand.

◆ In a bowl, mix together the curry powder and the fromage frais. Spread a generous helping of this mixture on each slice of bread. Then add the chicken strips, sprinkle with almonds and raisins, and top with another slice of bread.

Arthur's Delight

INGREDIENTS

makes 4 sandwiches

8 slices whole wheat bread

7 ounces (200 g) Roquefort cheese

Butter (optional)

3½ ounces (100 g) walnuts

7 ounces (200 g) grapes

Preparation Time • 5 minutes

◆ Toast the bread until crispy.

◆ Mix together the butter and Roquefort in a bowl if you prefer a softer texture.

◆ Use a crushing spell to roughly chop the walnuts.

◆ Rinse and dry the grapes and slice them in half.

◆ Spread each slice of bread with Roquefort, sprinkle with grape and walnut pieces, and top with another slice of bread.

Molly's Sweetie

INGREDIENTS

makes 4 sandwiches

4 eggs

8 lettuce leaves

2 carrots

8 slices of bread

2$^{1}/_{10}$ ounces (60 g) mayonnaise

Preparation Time • 10 minutes ◆ *Cooking Time* • 9 minutes

◆ Boil water in a small cauldron over high heat.

◆ When the first bubbles appear, carefully drop the eggs into the water and cook for 9 minutes.

◆ Rinse and dry the lettuce leaves and scrub, peel, and grate the carrots.

◆ Peel the eggs and slice with staccato flicks of your wand.

◆ Smear each slice of bread with mayonnaise then top with lettuce, eggs, and carrots before covering with a second slice of bread.

Bill's Treat

INGREDIENTS

makes 4 sandwiches

8 slices country bread

2$\frac{1}{10}$ ounces (60 g) butter

5$\frac{1}{3}$ ounces (150 g) arugula

½ bunch of radishes

8 slices roast beef (not too well-done)

Preparation Time • 5 minutes

◆ Cover each beautiful slice of bread with soft butter.

◆ Rinse the arugula. Wash and dry the radishes and remove the stems. Slice in rounds.

◆ Place one slice of meat on each slice of buttered bread, sprinkle with radish slices, and top with arugula and the final slice of bread.

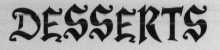

DESSERTS

Mrs. Weasley's desserts are always the best part of mealtime at The Burrow.

Burrow-Style Strawberry Ice Cream

EQUIPMENT
1 blender

Silicon tray(s) or mold(s) to hold
34 fluid ounces (1 l)

INGREDIENTS
makes 34 fluid ounces, 1 l

18 ounces (500 g) strawberries

7 ounces (200 g) powdered sugar

Juice of 1 lemon

8 ½ fluid ounces (250 ml)
whipped cream

Perfect for an end-of-summer celebration!

Preparation Time • 10 minutes + *Resting Time* • 5 hours

◆ Remove the garden gnomes from the strawberries then rinse and hull them (the strawberries, not the gnomes).

◆ Blend together the fruit, sugar, and lemon juice or cast a mixing spell on them.

◆ Next add the whipped cream, gently incorporating it in order to keep as much air in your mixture as possible. (You may skip this step if you have mastered the frothing spell.)

◆ Pour the mixture into the tray or molds in the shape of your choice then chill for at least 5 hours.

Rhubarb Pie and Custard

EQUIPMENT
1 tart pan 8½ inches (22 cm) in
   diameter

INGREDIENTS
serves 6

For O.W.L. Level Wizards:
1 shortcrust pastry

18 ounces (500 g) rhubarb
   compote

3½ ounces (100 g) brown sugar

¾ ounce (20 g) butter

1 container vanilla custard
   (4 ounces)

1 tablespoon milk

For N.E.W.T. Level Wizards:

Dough:
3½ ounces (100 g) softened
   butter

1¾ ounces (50 g) powdered sugar

7 ounces (200 g) flour

Pinch of salt

1 egg

Filling:
2⅕ pounds (1 kg) rhubarb

3½ ounces (100 g) brown sugar

¾ ounce (20 g) butter

Custard:
4 egg yolks

4 Ð ounces (125 g) sugar

1 vanilla bean

17 fluid ounces (½ l) milk

*You'll eat so much of this tasty dessert,
you'll need to loosen your waistband.*

Preparation Time • 30 minutes   ◆   *Cooking Time* • 45 minutes

Preparation of the dough for N.E.W.T. level wizards:
◆ Don't let yourself be distracted by the cries of the ghoul in the
attic and mix the softened butter and sugar together in a bowl.
Beat together with a mixing spell until the mixture is creamy.
Then add the flour and a pinch of salt. Mix again in the opposite
direction of the sun's path and incorporate the egg (no shell).

◆ Form a thick disk and let it rest for 15 minutes in the
refrigerator.

◆ Prepare the rhubarb filling: cut off the ends, and only peel if
the branches are very large and stringy. Use sharp swipes of your
wand to cut the rhubarb into small pieces. Place the rhubarb
pieces in a standard model cauldron along with a small glass of
water, the sugar, and butter. Cover and heat for 15 minutes over
low heat.

For all wizards:
◆ Preheat your oven to 350°F (180°C, th. 6–7).

◆ Lay the pie dough into the pan, prick the bottom with a fork
(or the tip of your wand, making sure to clean it afterwards), pour
in the compote, spread out the filling evenly, and bake for 45
minutes.

Preparation of the custard for N.E.W.T. level wizards:
◆ Beat together the eggs and sugar.

◆ Slice the vanilla bean in half lengthwise then remove the seeds
with the back of your knife or with a swipe of your wand. Add the
vanilla seeds to the above mixture.

◆ Place a small cauldron over low heat and warm the milk: it
should be hot but not boiling. Remove from heat and pour the
milk over the eggs, whisking vigorously, then return this mixture

(continued)

to the cauldron and cook for 5 minutes over very low heat, stirring constantly with a spoon made of white birch wood and never letting it boil.

◆ Coat the spoon by stirring the custard then press your finger to the back of the spoon, leaving a mark. If the imprint is still visible when you remove your finger, the custard is ready.

Preparation of the custard for O.W.L. level wizards:
◆ Stir together the milk and vanilla custard and heat in a small cauldron or with a dragon-breath spell.

For all wizards:
◆ Serve the rhubarb pie with warm custard and enjoy in good company.

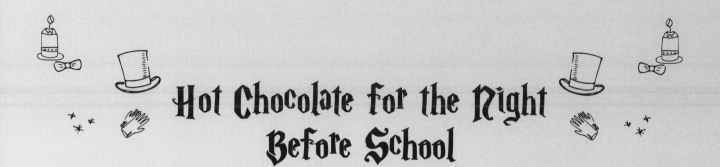

Hot Chocolate for the Night Before School

INGREDIENTS

serves 6

17 fluid ounces (½ l) milk

3¹/₅ ounces (90 g) honey

3¹/₅ ounces (90 g) cocoa

18 ounces (500 g) whipped cream

Preparation Time • 10 minutes

◆ Pour the milk into a small cauldron. Add the honey and warm slightly.

◆ Add the cocoa with a twirl of your wand and gently stir, holding your wand in your left hand.

◆ Top with whipped cream and serve immediately.

UNOFFICIAL RECIPES INSPIRED BY

THE NOBLE HOUSE OF BLACK

Soup for the Basilisk

EQUIPMENT
1 blender

Don't be afraid to lock eyes with this soup!

INGREDIENTS
serves 4

1 large bunch of watercress (if out of season, use other kinds of greens)

2 medium potatoes

34 fluid ounces (1 l) water, separated

4 eggs

1 black olive

Preparation Time • 10 minutes • *Cooking Time* • 45 minutes

◆ Kreacher rinses the watercress, breaking and removing the thick stalks.

◆ Then he washes the potatoes, peels them, and cuts them using a cut-all spell.

◆ Kreacher will gather water and heat it in a large cauldron. When large bubbles appear, he will add the potatoes to the water and let them cook for 35–40 minutes until the point of a knife can easily poke through. Then he adds the watercress and continues cooking 5 more minutes before putting everything in the blender. (Kreacher knows what he must do: Soup for the Basilisk must be as green as the Great Serpent's scales.)

◆ Kreacher boils more water in a smaller cauldron and cooks the eggs for 9 minutes exactly.

◆ Kreacher removes the eggs from the water and places them under a stream of cold water right away to crack their shells. He peels the eggs and cuts them open to remove the yolks, taking care to preserve their round shape. (Kreacher knows his masters will pay close attention to this detail.)

◆ Next, he cuts off one side of the egg yolk, so it will stay in place on the serving dish. He cuts the olive in thin slices.

◆ Kreacher places the egg yolk in the center of a shallow bowl featuring the coat of arms of his masters' family. Then he pours the soup into the bowl until it covers the bottom half of the yolk, places an olive slice on top of the yolk to resemble the Basilisk's eye, and serves it hot.

Roasted Hippogriff and Potato Puree

EQUIPMENT
4 sheets of parchment paper

INGREDIENTS
serves 4

2⁴/₅ ounces (80 g) butter

10²/₃ ounces (300 g) pieces of freshly executed hippogriff (or 14 ounces (400 g) stir-fried ostrich) (see section on Shopping)

10²/₃ ounces (300 g) black trumpet mushrooms

1 onion

Salt, pepper

2¹/₁₀ ounces (60 g) redcurrant jelly

14 ounces (400 g) purple potatoes

3½ ounces (100 g) crème fraîche

It's probably best that Buckbeak is kept in his room when Kreacher is making this recipe . . .

Preparation Time • 30 minutes • Cooking Time • 25 minutes

◆ Kreacher begins by tossing a little butter into a pot and quickly frying the pieces of hippogriff (or ostrich) over very high heat to brown them on all sides.

◆ Then Kreacher cleans the black trumpet mushrooms with a damp cloth. The mushrooms should not be soaked—they will absorb water and the masters do not like that at all.

◆ Kreacher peels the onion without crying and cuts it in thin slices.

◆ Kreacher lays out large sheets of parchment paper and transfers a few pieces of hippogriff to each one, surrounding the meat with mushrooms and onions. He also adds salt, pepper, a pat of butter, and never forgets the spoonful of redcurrant jelly.

◆ Next, Kreacher closes the parchment paper parcels by folding the paper together and then folding over a small band two fingers wide. He folds down another band the same size, creating a kind of envelope, so that all of the wonderful aromas will stay locked inside the paper.

◆ Kreacher puts the parcels in the oven and cooks them for 25 minutes at 350°F (180°C, th. 6–7)

◆ While the hippogriff (or ostrich) is cooking, Kreacher washes, peels, and slices the potatoes. He cooks them for 40 minutes in a large cauldron of boiling water until they can be easily pierced with a knife.

◆ Then Kreacher purées the potatoes and adds the crème fraîche.

◆ Kreacher serves the meat with the black trumpet mushrooms, purple purée, and the sauce as red as hippogriff's blood.

◆ The masters are satisfied with Kreacher's cooking—they have never given him clothes.

Mudblood Crunch

EQUIPMENT

4 cake rings, 3 inches (8 cm) in diameter (see chapter on Techniques for Non-Magical People)

1 piping bag (see chapter on Techniques for Non-Magical People)

INGREDIENTS

serves 4

7 ounces (200 g) shortbread cookies

7 ounces (200 g) dark chocolate

7 ounces (200 g) sweetened whipped cream

1 jar black cherries in syrup

Preparation Time • 10 minutes + 15 minutes of resting time
Cooking Time • 15 minutes

◆ Kreacher begins by squashing the shortbread cookies in a bowl until he has made a very fine powder.

◆ Next, he places the cake rings on plates and packs the cookie crumbs inside to form a pedestal like those on the statues honoring the glory of his masters. Then he chills the plates for 15 minutes.

◆ Kreacher carefully melts the chocolate and allows it to cool slightly. He mixes it with the whipped cream, adds sugar if necessary, and places it in the refrigerator with the cookie crumb bases.

◆ Now Kreacher drains the cherries. He keeps the juice and boils it at high heat in a small cauldron for 15 minutes until it becomes thick and syrupy.

◆ Kreacher takes the cookie crumb bases out of the refrigerator, removes the cake rings, and places the cherries on top of the cookie crumbs in a circle, as one might on a tart.

◆ Then Kreacher takes the piping bag, fills it with the chocolate whipped cream, and pipes small chocolate domes on top of the cherries that are as venerable as the intellect of his masters.

◆ He now places more cherries on top of his chocolate cream domes, pressing down a little to keep them from falling off, and finishes his work with a spoonful of syrup over each of the desserts for his noble masters.

◆ This dessert is the favorite of the very noble and very ancient family who are Kreacher's masters.

Dementor's Kiss (alcohol free)

INGREDIENTS

serves 6

10¹⁄₁₀ fluid ounces (30 cl) ice
  cold mint syrup

34 fluid ounces (1 l) lemon juice

A chilling drink, much like the effect of the dementors.

Preparation Time • 2 minutes

◆ Kreacher pours the syrup into the beautiful glasses of his masters and dilutes it ever so slightly with the lemon juice to keep the color as murky and greenish as possible.

◆ The masters like it when Kreacher serves them this drink on ice.

Elf Wine (alcohol free)

INGREDIENTS

serves 4

I orange

17 fluid ounces (50 cl) grape
    juice

10¹/₁₀ fluid ounces (30 cl) water

4 tablespoons brown sugar

Handful of blueberries (frozen if
    out of season)

I teaspoon ground ginger

I teaspoon ground nutmeg

I cinnamon stick

I star anise, whole

Perfect for toasting to the Dark Lord.

Preparation Time • 5 minutes + 1 hour of resting time
Cooking Time • 5 minutes

◆ With a sharp knife, Kreacher skins the orange and cuts the flesh
into quarters.

◆ Beginning with a blood-red grape juice, he pours all of the
ingredients into a cauldron, boils the mixture for 5 minutes, then
removes the cauldron from the fire and allows it to rest for
I hour, stirring occasionally.

◆ After this, Kreacher filters the mixture and serves it hot or
cold, depending on the desires of his masters.

INDEX BY RECIPE

SHOPPING

INGREDIENTS

The **jellies**, **cranberry chutney**, **mincemeat**, **golden syrup** (molasses), **cream soda**, and **butterscotch©** can be found in most supermarkets, particularly in the "international" section.

The **pudding mixes** as well as the **candied orange peels** are hiding on the baking aisle.

Fennel seeds are located in the spice section of most grocery stores.

Lemongrass, **dog rose**, and **elderberry flowers** can be picked up from an herbalist or purveyors of organic foods.

True Nopal© **cactus water** can be found in most grocery stores or online at *Amazon.com*

You can find **ostrich** meat online from Fossil Farms at *https://www.fossilfarms.com/ostrich-meat*.

If you do not want to use ostrich, beef or lamb has a similar taste, or use smoked (or regular) turkey meat.

MOLDS AND COOKIE CUTTERS

Chocolate frogs: search online for "chocolate frog mold" or go to *Amazon.com*

Licorice wands: molds for cake edges in the shape of ropes are sold with chocolate and fondant products in stores specializing in pastry materials.

Search online for "rope cake mold" or go to Amazon.com.

Bone molds: search online for Wilton© brand molds or go to *Amazon.com*

Cookie cutters: search online for "lizard cookie cutters" or go to *Amazon.com*

IMPORTANT:

The names and addresses of these products are presented for informational purposes only.

This book is not intended to serve as an advertisement for any brands, boutiques, or websites. This list is not exhaustive and is provided ex gratia to help the readers of this book in their search for ingredients and materials.

The author has no influence over product availability and is not responsible for potential problems that may occur in the process of ordering them.

Conversion Charts

Metric and Imperial Conversions

(These conversions are rounded for convenience)

Ingredient	Cups/Tablespoons/Teaspoons	Ounces	Grams/Milliliters
Butter	1 cup/ 16 tablespoons/ 2 sticks	8 ounces	230 grams
Cheese, shredded	1 cup	4 ounces	110 grams
Cream cheese	1 tablespoon	0.5 ounce	14.5 grams
Cornstarch	1 tablespoon	0.3 ounce	8 grams
Flour, all-purpose	1 cup/1 tablespoon	4.5 ounces/0.3 ounce	125 grams/8 grams
Flour, whole wheat	1 cup	4 ounces	120 grams
Fruit, dried	1 cup	4 ounces	120 grams
Fruits or veggies, chopped	1 cup	5 to 7 ounces	145 to 200 grams
Fruits or veggies, pureed	1 cup	8.5 ounces	245 grams
Honey, maple syrup, or corn syrup	1 tablespoon	0.75 ounce	20 grams
Liquids: cream, milk, water, or juice	1 cup	8 fluid ounces	240 milliliters
Oats	1 cup	5.5 ounces	150 grams
Salt	1 teaspoon	0.2 ounce	6 grams
Spices: cinnamon, cloves, ginger, or nutmeg (ground)	1 teaspoon	0.2 ounce	5 milliliters
Sugar, brown, firmly packed	1 cup	7 ounces	200 grams
Sugar, white	1 cup/1 tablespoon	7 ounces/0.5 ounce	200 grams/12.5 grams
Vanilla extract	1 teaspoon	0.2 ounce	4 grams

Oven Temperatures

Fahrenheit	Celsius	Gas Mark
225°	110°	1/4
250°	120°	1/2
275°	140°	1
300°	150°	2
325°	160°	3
350°	180°	4
375°	190°	5
400°	200°	6
425°	220°	7
450°	230°	8

Techniques for Non-Magical People

By Professor D. Eyewhy

COOKIE CUTTERS AND CAKE RINGS:

Create your own cookie cutters and cake rings by cutting out the shapes you need from a thin cardboard such as poster board. All you have to do is follow the line with the tip of a sharp knife and attach the ends with staples to create the shapes of your dreams.

PIPING BAGS:

The kitchens of non-magical people are overflowing with small and large freezer bags. Fill one of them two-thirds of the way and twist the top of the bag to seal it. Cut off one of the corners.

If you want to use a special piping tip, don't forget to put it in the bag before you fill it. Believe me, things will be so much easier if you do it this way.

SYRINGES AND OTHER PIPETTES:

Tiny syringes (without needles, of course) are available in pharmacies.

You can also use pipettes for liquid medications—the result is amazing!

MOLDS OF VARIOUS SHAPES:

Don't have the mold of your dreams? Don't panic! Make one with your own two hands out of homemade modeling clay!

Make your own modeling clay by mixing 1 glass of salt with 1 glass of water and 2 glasses of flour. Form your mold and dry for one or two hours, depending on how damp your clay is. Then microwave it in 1-minute intervals at low power until it hardens. When you are ready to use your mold, line it with microwave safe plastic wrap for cold fillings and parchment paper for warm fillings.

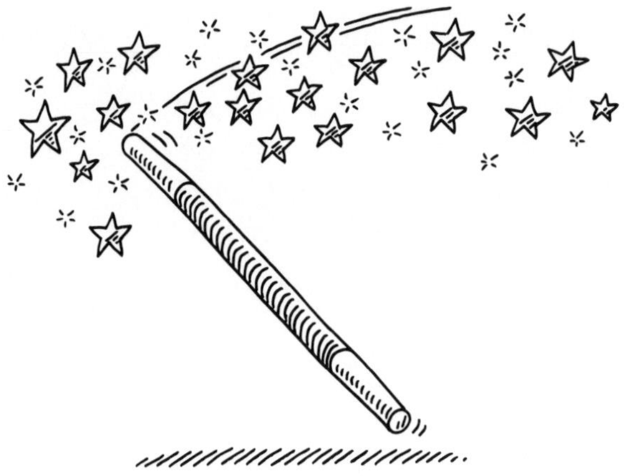